What people are saying about...

Catholics in Crisis?

"In his usual thought-provoking yet popular style, Father Bausch challenges readers to observe the signs of the times and develop effective pastoral approaches to meet the spiritual needs of a generation in need of evangelization and catechesis. Although not without some controversial and debatable statements, this book makes a contribution to the necessary dialogue regarding contemporary religious culture."

✝ Most Reverend John M. Smith
Bishop Of Trenton

"Here Father Bausch presents an amazing amount of research in an engaging and lively manner. His succinct and cogent analysis of the New Age is an exercise in clarification of what is so appealing and what is so dangerous about it to a healthy Christian faith. His treatment of fundamentalism is balanced and incisive.... This book deserves a wide audience."

Gloria Durka, Ph.D.
Professor, Fordham University

"Always the positive pastor, Bausch's sixteen suggestions for shaping a vital church is worth the price of the book itself. It is a blessing to the church at large that Bill Bausch continues to share his wisdom, commitment, and practical experience so fully and freely."

Robert L. Kinast, Director
Center for Theological Reflection

"How easily we say 'Read the Signs of the Times,' all the while knowing it takes special skills. William Bausch has them. He knows our culture: TV personalities, sociologists, New Age authors and the rest. He also has his ear to the ground when it comes to church matters. Thus, he brings much to a reflection on Catholics in crisis. Best of all you will come away not just enlightened but hopeful."

Rev. Frank McNulty
St. Teresa of Avila, Summit, NJ

CATHOLICS IN CRISIS?

The Church Confronts Contemporary Challenges

WILLIAM J. BAUSCH

TWENTY-THIRD PUBLICATIONS
Mystic, CT 06355

Second printing 1999

Twenty-Third Publications
185 Willow Street
P.O. Box 180
Mystic, CT 06355
(860) 536-2611
(800) 321-0411

ISBN: 0-89622-965-3
Library of Congress Catalog Card Number: 98-61592
Printed in the U.S.A.

For Madeline Tibbitt
on her eightieth birthday

wife, mother,
servant of the Church
leader in the Church
prophetess
the valiant woman

Contents

Introduction

There are contemporary challenges and influences on Catholic life in this day and age that we can hardly duck. Thus I have written this "primer" for Catholics and others who share concerns about these influences. The New Age, covered in chapters one and two, is surely an influence that is so pervasive and part of the culture that many Catholics are "into" it, often even without realizing it. New Age is so concrete, so appealing, so sentimental—and so fuzzy. It has something to offer, but included in its offerings are dangers to a healthy and balanced Christian faith and so it's worth examining.

The third and fourth chapters deal with fundamentalism, its phenomenal success and inroads among Catholics. They examine its beginnings, failures, successes, and its vast appeal. These chapters also deal with fundamentalist teaching and how Catholics, quite susceptible to it because of their own religious illiteracy, can respond to it—and learn from it.

The fifth and sixth chapters deal with the apocalyptic themes of the end of the world and the second coming of Christ, themes carefully marketed as we approach the year 2000 but definitely worth examining even as we enter a new millennium. Here we are introduced to the esoteric language and often outrageous prophets of apocalypticism. But, far more importantly, here too we can learn something about a part of our tradition that we would prefer to forget and often dismiss in practice, and therefore wind up cutting ourselves off from a major theme of revelation. So an examination of apocalypticism has a value far beyond any current hoopla or any magic number with three zeros.

It is no secret that much of the success of both New Age and fundamentalism has been at the expense of the Catholic church, which indeed is a troubled church. It is no secret that the Catholic church is in crisis, not only over the notable issues of sex and authority, but also over the very issue of credibility. The all-too-common cry of the young is "I believe in God but I don't believe in the church."

The church today is badly hemorrhaging. In Europe many Catholic churches and monasteries are now restaurants or museums. In Latin American vast numbers have converted to Protestant fundamentalist religions. Even in Catholic Ireland and Quebec, church influence and attendance is dwindling. In the United States church attendance has dropped to twenty-five percent. The percentage of U.S. Hispanics/Latinos who describe themselves as Catholics has dropped from seventy-eight percent in the early 1970s to sixty-seven percent today. There is a critical shortage of priests and a drop in the numbers of seminarians. It is a troubled church indeed.

Chapter seven therefore steps back to examine the internal and external reasons for this weakness, for the leakage, loss, and internal strife that are well documented. What caused this? How did it happen to a church once so powerful and prestigious? Is there hope? What might be our strategies for restoration during a new millennium? The response to this last question slides us into chapter eight, a kind of extended "afterword." I should have stopped the book at chapter seven, but, unrepentant pastor that I am, I could not resist hazarding some ways we might respond and rebound. It's only guesswork, but I felt I had to try.

This book, then, is meant to be expository, trying its best

to give an account of the New Age, fundamentalism, and apocalypticism, but always with an eye to increasing our understanding of these movements, learning from them, and sending us back to our own tradition to see what we've missed, what we've overlooked. To this extent I usually take a pro-con approach: I look at what's wrong with these movements, but also what, even in a backhanded way, is right with them and what they have to say to us.

The overall thrust of this book is caught well in the observations of Michael Paul Gallagher:

> When people find themselves "sated but unsatisfied" by the old materialism, as well as bored or untouched by their experience of church, they can enter a new search without anchors. It is that drifting that constitutes a danger: the hunger is good but insofar as the lived culture weakens people's Christian roots, such a spiritual quest leaves itself open to becoming a mixture of ancient heresies like gnosticism and pelagianism. In a context of religious malnutrition, such lonely spirituality easily becomes another form of de-christianization. Without community and contemplation, it risks being a narcissism without Christ. In fact this phenomenon seems the product of the two elements already described: where church discourse fails to connect with human needs and where culture gradually forces religious consciousness into the realm of the private, then fundamental spiritual hungers in people remain unsupported and yet desperate in their longing for some kind of food. Thrown back on their own resources, people express their suppressed religiousness in different ways which can range, depending largely on temperament, from so-called New

Age explorations to more fundamentalist rigidities.
—*Clashing Symbols*, Paulist Press, 1998, p. 114

Who might benefit from this book? I would suggest mentors and candidates for the RCIA as a part of their overall education into the church and the dangers to be aware of in their newfound faith. Secondly, those engaged in evangelization programs will, I hope, find the material useful. Thirdly, homilists will find much data that is a rich resource for preaching on the themes of this book. Finally, I suggest that small faith-sharing groups, study groups, classroom and adult education facilitators might find this book helpful. It's not that they will agree with everything herein, but that they might simply find the information challenging enough to disagree, discuss, and come to their own conclusions about whether we Catholics are in crisis and whether we can respond accordingly.

1

The New Age

My true definition of wholistic health is what people
commonly call miracles. But there are no miracles.
We lift the veil of illusion of the physical senses and see
ourselves in the purity, the wholeness of our true being.

—New Age practitioner

A Philadelphia lawyer, browsing in a bookstore, picked up
a biography of Jack Kerouac, whom people in the 60s certainly remember as the poet laureate of the Beat Movement.
The lawyer discovered, to his surprise, that Kerouac was
deeply moved, of all things, by the story of St. Thérèse and
her "shower of roses." As a Catholic he knew, of course, that
the Little Flower promised to send a "shower of roses" on
those who asked her help, but he was surprised that she fig-
ured in Kerouac's life. Although he himself was a child of
the 60s, he was now a man of the 90s, so he thought the
shower of roses was a nice "metaphor." But then he goes on
to tell this story:

> I remember during World War II that my father,
> a naval surgeon, was thought to have been a
> casualty during an amphibious landing in the
> Pacific. My mother gathered the family together
> and began a novena to St. Thérèse. The very
> next day, the doorbell rang and there stood a

neighbor—it was winter of 1945—with a dozen long-stemmed roses. He hadn't heard that my father was missing; he knew nothing of our prayers, he just thought our family would like the flowers. Were the roses just a coincidence? Was the neighbor's gift a fluke? My mother, who shortly afterwards learned that my father was alive, believed to the end of her days that the bouquet of roses did not happen by chance. It was, as she always described it, a sign.

It's this kind of thing that is now being taken seriously, an accepted sense of the paranormal, the supernatural, saints and angels, roses and crystals, and all the rest. It's a sign that the New Age has arrived. "New Age" is a term coined by the spirit medium "Alice Bailey" of the Theosophical Society of America who died in 1949. The term became common parlance after the musical "Hair." It is now a catch-all phenomenon that presents an alternate way of looking at things, a kind of different map from the normative secular one current in America.

Not surprisingly, New Age's immediate roots, like so much else, lie in the 60s and early 70s, when vast social and scientific changes were being made. The old order was collapsing, and people were looking for answers to life, but no longer in the old established religions; they were looking outside them. It was a widespread phenomenon, happening for example in the world of business where Stephen Covey offered his seven habits of highly successful people. It was happening in medicine where the old ways were challenged and the interaction between spirit and matter was more and more explored by people like Bernie Siegel, Herbert Benson, and Dean Ornish. The latter writes this in his best-seller, *Love and Survival:*

Love and intimacy are at the root of what makes

us sick and what makes us well, what causes sadness and what brings happiness, what makes us suffer and what leads to healing. If a new drug had the same impact, virtually every doctor in the country would be recommending it for their patients. It would be malpractice not to prescribe it—yet with few exceptions, we doctors do not learn much about the healing power of love, intimacy, and transformation in our medical training. (p. 3)

He goes on to point out that the *New England Journal of Medicine* says that more money is spent out of pocket for alternative medicine than for traditional medicine—even though most insurance companies do not yet cover these costs.

There are indeed countless books on alternate medicine, alternate psychotherapy, alternate addiction movements like the twelve steps, men's, women's, human potential, etc., movements. All add up to an interest in healing, transformation, and spirituality not happening within traditional synagogues, temples, and mosques. New Age, in this sense, becomes a kind of alternate pseudo religion. In fact, straightforwardly, they, the New Agers, declare that the time of rationalism, materialism, and atheism is over. Now is the time of "pure spiritualism." But again, this is not the spiritualism of the old "age of Aries" (Judaism), or the old dogmatic "age of Pisces" (Christianity). (Pisces, by the way, is the Latin word for fish, and the fish was the secret code symbol among early Christians to identify one another.) Rather, it is the "Age of Aquarius" where you realize that you are God.

A Vast Influence

This New Age is vast. I'm a computer nerd, so I looked up the New Age on the web site and found 7,911,603 documents about New Age including Cyber Psychic readings, herbs and vitamins, psychic development, planet signs in the house, skull capacity, monthly horoscopes, past life-times, Tarot chat room, spell kits, magic oils, crystal balls, UFO sightings, pagan alternate spirituality, and angelnet—to mention just a few! New Age bookstores (like the one that just opened up in my small town) and newspapers are found everywhere.

The channeled sayings of "Lazaris" and "Ramtha" are pop-ular, their thrust esoteric: New Agers are trying to align themselves to a world moving through a "precession of equinoxes" towards the age of Aquarius. (As we shall see in another chapter, they are right in line with the evangelical Christians in their vision of world "purification" trial, and the arrival of a new world order.)

And they have their "scripture," believe in ongoing reve-lation, and stress experience rather than theological reason-ing. And they have their own language: aromatherapy, ayurveda, centering, integrated energy therapy, neuro-lin-guistic programming, tai chi, reflexology, reiki, yoga, and so on. New Age books with titles like *Saved by the Light; Anatomy of the Spirit: The Seven Stages of Power and Healing; Touching Spirit: A Journal of Healing and Personal Resurrection; 100 Ways to Attract Angels; 101 Ways to Avoid Reincarnation: Or Getting It Right the First Time; Abduction: Human Encounters With Aliens; Advent Calendar for the Salvation of the Planet;* and *Agartha: A Journey to the Stars* are all unbearably simplistic and accepted at face value. Nevertheless, they are long on the bestseller lists, and New Age music is a billion dollar industry. In fact, the sales of New Age books have surged from $5.6 million in 1992 to over $10 million today. Sales of natural products have surged from $4.2 billion in 1990 to $14 billion in 1996, and the sales of organic foods have risen from $1 billion in 1990 to $3.5 billion in 1996. British sociologist David Martin critiques all of this well:

> Nearly every bookstore today has a section given over to "spirituality." Spirituality is one of those words, like metaphysics and mysticism, that retain serious connotations but have looser usages referring to the psychic junk-shop. This is where popular semi-educated mentality browses over science fiction, television and cinematic fantasy about Ascended Masters and menacing Aliens, the offerings of Sunday-supplement anthropology, spiritual travelogues among the arcane and exotic, and alternative therapies, as well as pseudo-scholarly forays into the worlds of the gospels, the Gnostics, the Dead Sea Scrolls. All this can be complemented by down-market appropriations of words like "indeterminacy," "model," "trauma," "relativism," and other vague echoes from serious critiques of objectivity, positivism, and the concepts of truth and factuality. At the wackier margin lie notions like "identity-based knowledge," according to which individuals or groups tell equally "authentic" stories, as well as abuse of science as masculine, ego-based, ethnocentric, and exploitative. In short, located here is a riotous unreason at least as virulent as the crass scientism that dismisses all signals of transcendence as mere superstition on a par with the tooth fairy.

> —*Times Literary Supplement,* 8/29/97

The irony is that all of these artifacts and books and their messages appear to be so new but in reality they are all so very old, for many of the products, cures, and philosophies of the New Age have their origins in the practices of primitive cultures. A sociologist of religion, Robert Ellwood, describes it this way: New Age is "a contemporary manifestation of a western alternative spirituality going back at least to the Greco-Roman world." True enough. At the "Whole Life Expo" in October 1997, which packed more than 20,000 people into an arena in Austin, Texas, there were offered such things as Siberian shamanism, telepathic healing, trance dancing, past-life regression, spirit walking, aura reading, herbalism, and aromatherapy—all ancient techniques.

Life-Force Therapy

A good example of what happened there is the seminar presented by psychotherapist Bradford Keeney who lived and studied the healing practices of the Kalahari Bushman, the Australian Aborigine, and the South American Guarani, among others. In a remarkable presentation Keeney demonstrated to some two hundred attendees how he marshals and uses "life-force energy." While the rest of the crowd dances to taped tribal drums, many people Keeney touches either pass out or fall to the floor. "We live in an ocean of energy" he says as he moves through the enraptured crowd. "It's joy, it's ecstasy, it's being fully alive."

And all this is not to mention the phenomenal male "Promise Keepers" who have met in stadiums by the millions and the female "Women of Faith" (founded by Stephen Arterburn of the New Life Clinics), who recently, at ten thousand strong, joined more than two hundred thousand other women at the Continental Arena in East Rutherford, New Jersey—and paid $39 for their seats. They were Catholic, Baptist, Presbyterian, Episcopalian, and Lutheran, and they were there to "bring back joy to their lives" and listen to Barbara Johnson and buy her books and tapes on spiritual advice.

The young, severed long ago from their own traditions, are especially attracted to New Age. At the Whole Life Expo

I just mentioned, it was noted that, as the report said—and I quote—"the crowd is heavy with folks wearing boat shoes and J. Crew shirts. The overflow throngs at the Austin expo are emphatically not wearing sarongs and they don't have full-body tattoos or multiple piercings. There is barely a dreadlock to be seen; the average age of the expo attendee is 38 and the average wallet is fat." So, many of our people are fascinated by the New Age, have read its books, and some, even those studying for Christian ministry, secretly dabble in New Age philosophy and wonder if somehow they can incorporate it into their traditional faith.

A Cafeteria Blend

So this New Age phenomenon, what is it? New Age is a cafeteria blend of some Eastern religious forms—most New Age teachers will appeal to the authority of an "ancient tradition" from which their teachings are derived—and western humanistic psychology, which emphasizes the positive, individualism, and the importance, even dominance, of self-esteem and self-fulfillment, as well as the subjective nature of reality. It is eclectic and outside the mainstream. It is as slippery and mutating as a chameleon and like the *Hero of a Thousand Faces*, it has a thousand expressions. Here are some of them.

There is, first of all, Neo-Orientalism which would include Buddhism, Hinduism, Hare Krishna (founded 1966), Transcendental Meditation (1959), and its endless cycle of reincarnations (people are their own god). This neo-Orientalism source reflects the upheavals of the 60s all over the world where, for example, student riots shut down the French government and our own students took over universities. The issues were the Vietnam war, racism, sexism, and a host of others. In a word, the counterculture had found the West wanting. It was socially and morally bankrupt, so after the tumultuous times of the 60s and 70s, the flower children having grown up and their communes all having failed, they turned to the East where people like Ram Dass and the various Maharajahs were ready to supply them with eastern forms of meditation and enlightenment.

Then there is Neo-paganism reflecting a return to pre-Christian roots, especially Celtic Europe with its Druids and Native North Americans with their reverence for the land. In this category too there is Wicca, a polytheistic religion, which ties into an interior power and white magic, that is, "good magic" connected with the earth spirit and plant spirit. And the feminist movement is here too, with its break away from patriarchal paradigms detected in Isis and Osiris of Egypt.

Then there is the category called Neo-Christian which involves an alternate reading of Christianity, such as the Unification Church (1954), whose founder Sun Myung Moon claims that Jesus appeared to him at age sixteen and gave him his mission; and Ways International (1957), founded by Victor Wierwille who claims God spoke to him in 1942. He teaches that Jesus is not God, there is no Trinity, and the Holocaust never happened. Further neo-Christian expressions would include the ill-fated David Koresh Branch Davidian group, Jim Jones' compound, and the teachings of The Celestine Prophecy. The Esoteric and Astral category of people claim that life is more than the technical, empirical reality that is offered by the secular world, as demonstrated by *channeling*, out-of-body experiences, reincarnation, astrology, and its astro-chat on the internet. UFOs and psychic readings, which are common among New Age practitioners, include reading others' "auras," energy readings, picking up one's vibrations, and numerology.

Selling Self-Improvement

The Self-Improvements category involves huge marketing and book sales that cover the areas of psychological and physical improvement. Devotees are particularly fond of Maslow's psychology with its concept of peak experiences. Such experiences, they say, help people to recognize their enlightenment and their divinity. New Age has mass-marketed the process of altered states of consciousness through relaxation techniques, behavior modification, deep meditation, visualization-imaging, etc.

There's Ron Hubbard's Scientology, which teaches that each person is a fallen immortal god who has been reincarnated over trillions of years; there is EST, founded by a car salesman, Jack Rosenberg of Philadelphia, who changed his name to Werner Erhard after changing it to Jack Frost. He says and I quote: "Self is all there is...You are god in your universe. You caused it." Some New Agers give evolution a new twist by teaching that the fall of man is due to his having sex with animals, thus producing the half-human, half-animal centaurs, minotaurs, and satyrs. (Never mind that there is no evidence of such, no bones yet found.) We evolve out of that fall through the realization of our divinity. And it goes on and on. Again, all these categories fall under the umbrella of what is referred to as the New Age, which borrows bits and pieces from all of these movements and religions and is a cover-all term for this spiritual smorgasbord. As Damien Thompson writes in his book *The End of Time:*

> In practice, the search for common denominators to New Age beliefs is often both daunting and unrewarding: daunting because they never stand still for long, and unrewarding because it seems pointless to analyze beliefs which are adopted and abandoned in such a capricious fashion. The somewhat blurred public perception of the New Age as a mixture of crystals, astrology, corn circles and Shirley MacLaine is not far from the truth: instead of a single corpus

of doctrine, the movement provides an arena in which apparently unconnected ideas and fads rub up against each other, often rather uncomfortably. The parameters of this movement can only really be measured by examining the range of material in a New Age bookshop; they are constantly shifting, as one fashion replaces another. Even sympathetic observers recognize a flavor-of-the-month quality to the way in which, for example, the passion for "channeling" and crystals has recently given way to an obsession with "Native American" wisdom...It is important here to distinguish between what the New Age claims to be, and what it actually is. On the rare occasions when it discusses its own lineage, it stresses the timeless quality of the beliefs it has inherited from the occult and from the cultures of India, China, and pre-Columbian America. It can be argued, however, that these borrowings (which tend to be carefully sanitized for modern Western tastes) are irrelevant to the true inspiration for the New Age, which is a belief in the emergence of a perfect world after a time of trial—in other words, the classic apocalypticism which Norman Cohn has dated back to ancient Iran and which entered Western culture with the Book of Daniel. This can take a millenarian form, where the new heaven and the new earth are expected to materialize at anytime, and believers are so overcome by this expectation that they reject all social and legal norms. But, as we have seen, there are many less virulent, though still powerful, forms of apocalypticism in which social conventions are respected but the enlightened live in the shadow—or the hope—of the end of this world.

—pages 195-196

New Agers are therefore as much excited by the year 2000 as are the most fervent Pentecostals.

Anyway, as we shall see, for all its shifting, borrowings, and fads, what the New Age doesn't borrow is the dogmatic, organizational, and ethical traditions of the religions. In a word, New Age is a blend of more standard religions while rejecting their wholes. And some do in fact find New Age helpful. But our question is: why the popularity of this non-organized "religion," this loosely connected, amorphous mix (psychic readings, tarot cards, yoga meditation, reiki, herbs, healing, crystals, astrology, angels, miracles, etc.)?

The one thing that all these diverse elements hold in common is that they are, as we said before, alternatives to the status quo. They are alternatives to a Christian worldview that has broken down, alternatives for a people to whom the gospel no longer speaks, alternatives for a people who, though affiliated, are religious illiterates, alternatives for people dissatisfied with the old Christian images of God who is presented as masculine, judgmental, angry, a cosmic policeman jealous of human potential, alternatives for people who find no satisfactory answers in their churches and are disenchanted with the lack of spirituality they find there. In fact, these "believers" claim that they represent the true teachings of Christianity which were lost or repressed by a misguided patriarchal and power-hungry church. This view is at the heart of James Redfield's best-seller, *The Celestine Prophecy*, which, incidentally, was on the *New York Times'* bestseller list for more than one hundred weeks.

So at this point we must take a closer look at this New Age phenomenon. I will offer eight serious critiques of New Age and then eight ways it can challenge us. Were I giving a lecture on this topic, I would not be so pedantic because among those attending the lecture, as I know from experience, are parents whose grown children are into New Age. Their children have left Catholicism or don't practice it (at least for the time being), and the parents are at least glad that their offspring are into "spirituality," are kind people who are living good lives. Any negative criticism makes them uneasy and even defensive. ("She's a good person. At least she meditates every day, which she never did before.") I would be sympathetic to such parents. They want and need guidance and reassurance, not condemnation or the word that their children are heretics. But, here, in the written word, in a book of explanations, we have to offer some insights into the fuzziness of the New Age movement and see that behind the affectations, pious practices, and sincerity, there really do lie serious theological problems that are hidden from people of good will, but which must be uncovered and discussed. So, we begin our eight critiques, saving our positive words for the next chapter.

Benign Heretics

1. First of all, New Agers are benign heretics. I say "benign" because, without the adjective, "heretics" sounds so harsh, and to use a politically incorrect word, judgmental, and, besides, most of them don't know it. But the fact is, being so eclectic, New Agers are bound to borrow the unorthodox as well. British sociologist David Martin again catches it nicely:

> In discussing the North American provenance.
> [Michael Brown, author of *The Channeling Zone*] reminds his readers that the United States is a land of exuberant religiosity where seven persons in ten believe in angels, five in ten in UFOs, and three in ten in reincarnation and communication with the dead. Beyond that, a

residue of Protestantism encourages do-it-your-self spiritual technology and individual experiment...For New Agers all truths are equal except the dogma that some truths are more equal than others. Where orthodox Christianity requires deliverance from evil into saving faith, New Agers seek out pathways where the innate goodness of humankind may flower in mutual harmony and respect for others and Nature. Worship is otiose when all you need is to adore your own divine humanity.

—*Times Literary Supplement,* 8/29/97

This "benign heresy" is expressed in any number of unofficial lists of beliefs (it has to be unofficial for New Age: anything official smacks of organization or rule setters), suggested to be common to New Agers, such as this one:

1. You are your own reality and destiny.

2. You have certain challenges to face and overcome in this lifetime. If you don't learn your lessons this time, you'll get them again.

3. We are not alone.

4. We are multidimensional beings currently having a human experience.

5. We are all receiving more help than we know, from angels, spirits, spirit guides, ascended masters, and others.

6. We can heal ourselves, our society, and our world.

In other words, New Agers are devotees of Monism which declares everything is one. They break down boundaries between themselves and the rest of reality. Some do this through drugs, others through meditation, especially Oriental meditation, some through breathing exercises (to get the oxygen high). The object of all this? To alter consciousness in order to experience everything as one, to lose the boundaries between themselves and others. This "everything is one" in turn translates as pantheism which means that everything is God, who is pure energy.

This is why New Agers are often into the ecology movement: not just to clean up the air we breathe, but because, as they see it, the air is them, the earth is them, the air is God and the earth is God and they are God. The earth is alive and even has a name, Gaia, which is the word for earth in Greek and the name of a Greek goddess. They even enlist science which says that people like Einstein with his famous formula of $E=MC^2$ backs them up. Energy equals mass plus the speed of light squared comes out as pure energy. This "pure energy" constitutes all of reality, which means that all reality is one. God is pure energy. God as pure energy is everything. I am God. This is Shirley MacLaine running along the seashore shouting, "I am God! I am God!"

Not for them the stance of classic theology which definitively speaks of an "Other." This Other is radically different from its creation and its creatures even though it is the ground of all that is (no Monism or Pantheism here). This Other moreover is personal and this Other calls, summons, confronts, and demands. We are answerable, under the judgment of the Other, and must conform. "Father, if you are willing, remove this cup from me, yet not my will but your will be done" (Luke 22:42).

So New Agers are Monists and Pantheists and that qualifies them as heretics.

No Room for Grace

2. In light of the above, our second point is: New Agers may also be considered Pelagians. New Age teachings, with their stress on radical individualism and self-determination leave no room for grace. New Agers can bring themselves to perfection, they can liberate the "angels" within themselves and the potential of the human mind can attain the "higher self." Salvation for them is basically, as we saw above, the self-awareness that they are God. If you want to see God, they say, look in the mirror. They therefore need no helping hand, no external grace, no personal God to assist. There is no sin to be redeemed from, only people less evolved. This is, of course, a far cry from the Christian dependency on God's unmerited grace in Christ.

3. New Agers are gnostics. They are heirs to the Gnosticism of the first centuries with which Christianity had to seriously contend. In fact, according to some scholars, many of the new religious and New Age movements are basically revivals of the Gnostic worldview, which is once more a competitor to Christianity as it was in St. Paul's and St. Augustine's time. Scholars describe Gnosticism as "a religious movement that stresses the need for salvation from the oppressive bonds of material existence, a salvation that is achieved, not by the grace of God, but rather by the individual's self-understanding or knowledge (gnosis) and effort" (John Saliba, *Understanding New Religious Movements*, page 29).

Scientology, for example, speaks of an extra-terrestrial who came to earth to free people from their bodies and to get back to the ideal and pure spiritual state. It's basically a Platonic dualism: Spirit vs. the material world, God and the universe, who would not accordingly soil himself directly with crass creation, so there are many intermediary spirits to deal with it, e.g. angels. You have soul vs. body, a divine spark waiting to be released from the prison of the body, a feat handled by a special revelation (gnosis), a secret, mystical enlightenment. Redemption, then, is not deliverance from sin and guilt, but a form of existential self-realization, that is, releasing the spark of the divine from the confines of the body by achieving awareness of the divine mysteries. In other words, the real problem in this world is that we are ignorant of our divinity. If only we realized that we are God and embraced the divinity within us, all would be solved. The primary striving of all New Agers, therefore, is enlightenment. That's the goal. There is no sin, no evil, no need of redemption, only, as we said, self-realization, the awareness, the enlightenment of who we are.

Moreover, if we fail to become enlightened, we will come back over and over again until we get it right, alternating between coming back as a man and a woman so we can experience the genius of both states (a departure from the parent Hindu form of recycling which has a man who has been bad coming back as a woman. Many New Age writers are women and would not, of course, countenance that disparity). And here we have another cornerstone New Age belief: reincarnation. We should not think, however, that New Agers imply that reincarnation means that one has done evil or committed sin to be atoned for in a new existence—there is no evil or sin, right or wrong—but rather, one has simply not learned one's lesson, one's "karma," of what it means to be a man or a woman. You'll come back over and over again until you learn your lesson and discover your divinity, your divine powers. "Karma," therefore, is not only evolution, but evolution forward. All of this contradicts the Christian understanding of creation, incarnation, redemption, and the Four Last Things.

Finding Their Center

4. New Agers are individualistic quietists in search of self-development. Salvation for them is finding their center. In

this they are, of course, only reflecting the general culture. It comes as no surprise, for example, that a July, 1998 *Wall Street Journal/NBC News Poll* finds that America's twenty-somethings, in listing their values, give patriotism a 55% importance rating (compared to a 75% rating for the 50- to 64-year-old group), a 53% importance rating for religion but a whopping 75% importance rating to the value of self-fulfillment.

It's no wonder that New Agers are weak on social justice. In its optimism about human potential, New Age is often blind to life's dark side. As a result of its focus on the self, New Age folk have little social conscience and seldom do they challenge social practices or personal behavior or address global evils. The transformation of the individual is their primary concern. Social responsibility finishes a poor second behind self-discovery. Besides, since the mind is the only or ultimate reality, issues of health, politics, and relationships have no meaning except at the spiritual level. As scholar Huston Smith pointed out in *Mother Jones*, "I am not sure how much social conscience there is in New Age thinking...Do New Age groups produce a Mother Teresa or a Dalai Lama?" Thus they are hardly in the tradition of Jesus and the prophets who would tell us that consciousness raising alone can't save us from evil and that salvation is not solely about self-transformation.

As Mary Pipher, author of *The Shelter of Each Other: Rebuilding Our Families*, writes:

> Therapy has contributed to the cultural shift from collective political action to individual. We've encouraged self-analysis at the expense of social change. I am reminded of a cartoon in which a person upset about famine in Ethiopia was told to take some Valium. At worst therapists have, to quote Ellen Goodman, "engaged in moral lobotomies." We have treated morality

> as a personal and pragmatic matter, not a community concern. We have abdicated our responsibility to speak to the moral and social issues of our times. —p. 125-126

In fact, if there is any common motif for New Agers it is therapy: personal therapy, feeling better, more powerful, more confident, more productive, more able to cope. Let me digress a bit and give you a very popular instance of the individualism of the New Age that matches perfectly the individualism of secular society. Look at the huge bestselling books on angels. They are literally and figuratively flying off the shelves. Not to mention TV shows, angel pins, calendars, plaques, and toys. People can't get enough of angels. But it's instructive to contrast the New Age view of angels (which matches perfectly our secular self-centeredness) and that of revelation reflected on and handed down by the tradition, the community of believers.

Seekers of Self-Fulfillment

The angels of the movies are seekers after self-fulfillment with sexual yearnings for humans. Movie critic Roger Ebert, in his review of the film *City of Angels,* notes:

> Angels are big right now in pop entertainment, no doubt because everybody gets one. New Age spirituality is me oriented, and gives its followers top billing in the soap operas of their own lives. People like to believe they've had lots of previous incarnations, get messages in their dreams, and are psychic. But according to the theory of karma, if you were Joan of Arc in a past life and are currently reduced to studying Marianne Williamson paperbacks, you must have made a wrong turn. When there's a trend toward humility and selflessness, then we'll

know we're getting somewhere on the spiritual front. That time is not yet. *City of Angels* hits the crest of the boom in angel movies—and like most of them it's a love story. Hollywood is interested in priests and nuns only when they break the vow of chastity, and with angels only when they get the hots for humans.

The angels of the best-sellers are, to put it bluntly, for the most part, personal genies, unpaid servants, who are there to give us what we desire, or, in the words of one author, Sophy Burnham, "to give us what we want." New Age angels figure as a kind of Santa Claus for grown ups. They change our tires on blustery wintery nights, rescue stalled motorists, protect people from gangs, comfort the grieving, and help mothers change the sheets on the bed. No wonder they are considered friendly and are welcomed. But in the community's record, the Bible, as you may have noticed, angels are not user-friendly. Rather they are considered dangerous and are not welcome at all. They do not provoke joy. On the contrary, if anything, they provoke fear. Gabriel, seeing that Mary, as a proper Jew, was scared out of her wits, had quickly to say, "Do not be afraid," and to dumbfounded Zechariah and the terrified shepherds, angels said "Do not fear."

Why the fear? Because in the Bible, you see, the visitation of an angel was not to change your tire on a wintery night, but to change you into changing the community! It was a signal that something profound, something perhaps even terrifying was about to happen for the whole people. "Do not be afraid," cautioned the angel to the shepherds of Bethlehem, "I am bringing you good news of great joy for all the people." The angel told Mary, for example, that she had been selected to change the world through the advent of the Messiah, and she finally answers, "This will be hard and I don't know what lies ahead, but let it be as you say," and she braced herself for Calvary. Angels are there to offer from God a transformation of lives and to turn people outward in service, not to enhance their productivity. If anything, they offer risk not comfort, like bringing burning coals to the lips of Isaiah and a dreadful journey to Abraham. Unlike the angels of the popular books, which are projections of our own self-need, the biblical angels come to summon, not always to serve. You see, there's the clash between the individual thought and the thought of the community's tradition. For New Agers, angels are viewed only as personal heavenly rescuers (and they sometimes are). For community folk, angels are viewed as messengers of risk and change and a call to profound holiness, well-springed in communal service.

Robert Wuthnow captures the distinction:

> As depicted in popular books and in our interviews, angels never scold. They give unconditional love. They have a good sense of humor. They also protect people, giving something to hope for or depend on when life seems like too much to handle on one's own. They appeal to populist or democratic strands in American culture: their existence cannot be proved or disproved by science, and thus experts may not have much to say about them; they appear to common people and, indeed, are thought to be ridiculed by people with education and positions of authority. They are also personal, serving, as one writer notes, as "Ethereal Secret Service agents" who protect people from danger. Yet they are often anonymous beings who make no demands and require no continuing relationship.
>
> Moreover, they are uninterested in theological

arguments, preferring just to perform random acts of kindness; indeed, they can conveniently be found in all religious traditions and even in the experiences of atheists and agnostics. Above all, they make for great stories and can be a source of fame and wealth if one chooses to write about them. But if seekers of the light are often finding little more than "spirituality lite," the fault is not entirely theirs. Spirituality has become big business, and big business finds many of its best markets by putting things in small, easy-to-consume packages. Few of the many angel books are long or difficult to read. They have wide margins, attractive pictures, and colorful stories. They are more likely to prick one's wallet than one's conscience.

—*After Heaven*, University of California Press, 1998, p. 132

No Organized Religion

5. Consistent with what we have just said our fifth point is New Agers have no room for organized religion. As one internet writer named Andrew Lutts put it:

The New Age movement itself is somewhat of a paradox, since to organize into some kind of "movement" could be considered contrary to the fundamentals of individual spiritual development. That is why there is some ambiguity to the meaning of the New Age, because it can mean different things to people. But that's okay. What is important is that each individual embarks on their own journey of learning, adventure, and discovery...Although it may be spiritual, New Age is far from being a formal religion. In fact, many New Agers tend to shy away from the structure and confines of traditional religious practices...The New Age person often prefers a direct spiritual experience rather than one from organized religion.

So, true to their individualism, New Agers have little or no room for any kind of relational faith, a faith necessarily honed, nourished, and critiqued by and within the community. So, for them, no assembly, no ecclesia, no church. "I don't believe in organized religion" is their cry. But as *Newsweek* (Oct. 20, 1997), slyly points out, "Anything that limits personal freedom is darkness—except for these seven spiritual laws, these ten celestine insights, this map of your erogenous zones...." Spirituality guru Deepak Chopra offers an appealing well-padded path to nirvana. "They say you have to give up everything to be spiritual," he says, "get away from the world, all that junk. I satisfy a spiritual yearning without making [people] think they have to worry about God and punishment."

There is something to be said for organized religion, although defending organized anything is a bold venture these days, but concerning organized religion we can at least respond that, while it is true that some atheists are more moral and decent and caring than some churchgoers, the fact is that as we face sickness and disappointment and betrayal, hurt and limitation, war, storms, natural disasters, and death, "religion" (to quote Rabbi Harold Kushner) "teaches us to face them in the company of others, our neighbors around us, and our ancestors before us who faced similar situations and left records of their experiences to enlighten and guide us." In short, we need a context of discernment and support. Organized religion has been there before and knows the pitfalls.

Reverse Fatalists

6. New Agers are reverse fatalists. If prosperity and health and such are the result of positive thinking, the poor and ill must be ignorant or lazy. If positive affirmations can cure illness, then those who are sick must feel guilty for not having enough faith. If loving thoughts heal, says New Age guru Louise Hay, the unhealed must have unloving thoughts. As she puts it, ear problems indicate there is something we don't want to hear, and eye problems tell us that we're not looking at some aspect of our life that we should, and heart attacks are brought on by our inability to love. So cancer, AIDS, starvation, and rape are basically choices we make at a conscious or unconscious level. Illness and injustice are ultimately the sufferer's own fault, thus adding emotional guilt to physical sickness.

So, when channeler Paul Tuttle was asked what would have been an appropriate New Age response to the Nazis, he responded, "The energy for Hitler's growth was resident in those victimized." (Don't you love the jargon?) In short, Hitler was the creation of those who died at his hand. This reminds me of the story of the son of Christian Scientist parents who asked his minister to pray for his father who was very ill. The minister remonstrated with the boy, telling him his father only thought he was sick, that his situation was an illusion based on his lack of faith. "Tell him to pray for faith." Later, the minister met the boy again and asked, "Does your father still think he's sick?" "No," the boy replied, "Now he thinks he's dead." Suffering is caused by our stars, bad karma, etc., and has no value. But for Christians, suffering can be redemptive.

7. Perhaps I should have put this first—New Agers are pragmatists. This is a variation on American individualism and consumerism. As John Shea reminds us, Americans live their lives a certain way and they need resources, not to change their lives to which they are addicted, but to cope. People

live at a very, very fast pace. People find themselves strung out and burned out, caught in choices they have made; I have no time; we don't even eat together; the fast track...demanding careers...cars for "families on the go," as one ad puts it. Human relationships, relationships with those nearest to us are stretched. And so it goes.

But word gets out that if you learn to access the spirit, if you learn to tap the center, you can continue your frantic pace and hectic way of life, and it won't do all the damage it's doing to you now! It's like Diet Coke: continue to drink and we'll take the fat-accruing calories out. So, the message is, you can continue to live at this speed without the cost. How? By means of "spirituality."

Spirituality becomes a means of gaining inner peace after you have squandered it so magnificently. Spirituality becomes a way that fast-paced people can continue their life, their "productivity," and not get burned out. It is a way they can enjoy the pleasures they want and stay in the fast lane, which they truly like because it brings other rewards like lots of toys and power. We work 160 hours more a year than twenty years ago, so they are not going to slow down, perish the thought. They would rather search for resources to find a center, a pause, a refreshment, inner peace. Hence yoga, meditation, Tai Chi, reiki: all are ways of finding the center without giving up the wrappings and trappings. New Age is the perfect movement for capitalism!

John Travolta, celebrity spokesman for the Church of Scientology, is a good example. Touting Scientology he says, "Through Scientology, you learn to examine your life and be more productive." Other devotees say that Scientology techniques help them communicate better and focus more clearly on their lives and careers, "approaches," as the *New York Times* article put it, that "stress philosophies and techniques intended to help people be more successful in the world in which they live, rather than concentrating on the afterlife"

(2/13/89) and rather than concentrating on community concerns.

No Room for Conversion

There's really no room for conversion in this scheme: no room for people who move into a radical lifestyle of service. Rather, in the New Age, St. Paul would have been a calmer, reasoned Pharisee; St. Francis would have been a happier, more productive merchant; Thomas Merton, a more centered student; Dorothy Day, an effective journalist; Mother Teresa, a smiling contemplative. New Agers don't hop the fast track and "leave all and follow me." No, they continue on the fast track with karma intact. And this may account for the popularity of New Age among Americans as well as anything.

8. Finally, as we hinted at previously, New Agers are dyed-in-the-wool endtime apocalyptics right in line with right wing fundamentalists who look at them with the same demeanor as the pope does Margaret Sanger. But they are united here. Because apocalypticism needs a wider context than I can give it here, I will reserve this critique for chapter five, "The End is Near."

So, there's our critique of the New Age: it is heretical, pelagian, gnostic, quietist, individualistic, pragmatic, and apocalyptic. Nor, finally, should we be adverse to declaring much of it "basic shallowness." Listen to Yale's notable scholar Harold Bloom:

> There is enormous difficulty in reading them [New Age books] whether one is reading poor Betty Eadie, or whether one is reading the distressingly sincere but incredibly boring Mr. Moody, whether indeed one is reading the inane Ariana Huffington, where the vacuity of the prose is so great that it's an incredible thing

to try to get through more than a couple of pages at a time and try to figure out what the lady thinks she means.

And concerning *The Celestine Prophecy*, that incredible best-seller, long on the *New York Times* Book list, Bloom says, "It is the most objectionable, the most absolute spiritual garbage that I believe I have seen in my entire life, and I have confronted a great deal of spiritual balderdash." That paragraph is putting it mildly. But he always hopes: "I suppose, though it may be self deluding on my part," says Bloom, "that in some sense I might reach some of those people, and get them to see that their concern or obsession with this is potentially of great value, but they are feeding themselves on McDonald's hamburgers rather than upon true nutriments" (Quoted in *Lingua Franca*, November 1996).

2

The Old Age

I choose my friends for their good looks, my
acquaintances for their good characters, and my enemies
for their intellects. One cannot be too careful in the choice
of his enemies.
—Oscar Wilde

How does the "Old Age" react to the New Age? In other
words, how do Catholic tradition and Catholic beliefs con-
front and learn from the New Age? For this chapter, then,
let's pick up on Bloom's phrase that ended the last chapter,
that the obsession with New Age is "potentially of great
value," and spend our time reflecting about how we community people, people of the church, can find what is good
in the New Age, or at least what it can say to us even in a
negative way. For we in the church have to dialogue with
these people. We must ask: how do organized religions deal
with a spiritually interested culture, to a self-centered spirituality being developed outside themselves? Thus, we offer
eight ways the New Age can provoke us.

1. First of all, the New Age phenomenon forces our attention to the radical shift in apologetics. Which is to say, that
even as short a time as twenty years ago, we were concerned with how to attract, talk to, and convince a population that had lost interest in religion and God, both of which
were considered quite irrelevant in the modern scientific
world. But not any more. Not any more. Today the interest

is definitely there. As an instance, in *America* magazine (October 12, 1994), editor Jim Martin tells of finding himself at Barnes & Noble where two hundred young, well-dressed people were gathered. He asked himself what they were there for: Tom Clancy? Anne Rice? John Grisham? No, they were there listening to best-selling author Mary T. Browne speaking about her best-selling book, *Mary T. Reflects on the Other Side.* He mused, ruefully, that any Catholic parish would give its right arm to have a group of two hundred young adults discuss the afterlife. Martin then read *Embraced by the Light* and *Saved by the Light,* two other very popular books. He comments:

> It is obvious why *Saved by the Light* and *Embraced by the Light* are so popular—they present comforting visions of the afterlife and answers to life's big mysteries. Yes, the answers are often ridiculously simplistic and much of what they say is outlandish. So it is tempting to snicker at their audiences and dismiss them... But it would be foolish to do so. For beyond their simplistic worldview, I suspect their attraction for some intelligent people is that they treat religious experience in a way that mainstream religious leaders often avoid.

He adds a postscript, "When I bought the two books, I told the goateed salesman at Barnes & Noble that I wanted to find out what made them so popular. As he wrapped up the books he said, 'Hope you like them. And, hey, you wanna read something else? Try angels. They're huge.' " What he is testifying to is that, nowadays, our apologetic thrust is to a clientele that is besotted with God, not the indifferent clientele of twenty years ago. There is today a massive soul search, a "widespread turning inward," as sociologist Wade Clark Roof puts it. Or, as Cyndee Miller puts it, "If the 80s were the decade when nothing was sacred, then this is the one when everything is."

And if you don't think so, note the enormous popularity of the *X-Files* whose opening trailer proclaims, "The Truth is out There"; CBS's *Touched by an Angel*; Hollywood's *The Preacher's Wife*, *Dear God*, and *Michael*; Dreamworks' *The Prince of Egypt* (the Moses story); *Kudan* and *Seven Years In Tibet*. Not to mention those nine thousand websites devoted to psychic and spiritual phenomena including: "The First Presbyterian Church of Elvis the Divine" (I kid you not); as well as 71,200 Christian internet sites and 27,000 Islam sites; perfumes named "Angel"; a car manufacturer whose motto is "Everything changes but the soul"; and the immense popularity of so-called "spiritual" writers like Deepak Chopra, Thomas Moore, M. Scott Peck, and Marianne Williamson. The fact is, post-modern culture is one of the most "God-interested" in history. These days we are indeed living in a secular society but a spiritual culture. "I consider myself to be spiritual but not really religious," is the prevailing statement.

The Search for God

The first "benefit" then of the New Age, of alternate religion, if you will, is to remind us forcefully of the earnest, insistent search for God. The "God is Dead" of the 70s is the "God is Alive" of the 90s. There is therefore fertile ground for religion. There's a field out there to plow. There is a hunger to be fed, and the New Age has forcefully reminded us of that. Our apologetic thrust is not to unbelievers but to believers, believers who in fact believe too much! Check this: according to a Time/CNN poll published in 1997, sixty-four percent of Americans now believe that creatures from elsewhere in the universe have recently been in personal touch with human beings. How do we reach such a post-modern, credulous people? As Michael Paul Gallagher puts it in his book

Clashing Symbols:

> We talk about the rise of secular culture, but we
> are witnessing a surprising turn-around in this.
> Years ago many sociologists argued confidently
> about an "irreversible secularization," predicting
> that religion would inevitably decline in influ-
> ence and become something socially marginal.
> More recently we have heard about the "return
> of religion," the rise of fundamentalism, the
> claims of faith within the public sphere, the
> multiplying of new religious movements, and
> the many-faceted spiritual exploration called
> "New Age." Strangely, both the floating reli-
> giousness and the fundamentalist rigidity may
> have the same origin, a desire to escape com-
> plexity and find anchors. These seemingly con-
> trary phenomena are provoked by the fragmen-
> tations, the malnutritions, and the rootless lone-
> liness of a dominantly secular culture. —page 6

2. The second benefit of the New Age—although "benefit"
may be ironic here—is that it forces us to ask, that if we
claim to have God, to possess a time-proven way of access
to the Divine in a fruitful and proven tradition—putting
aside the immediate question, why, then, do we not attract
more—we must move to the deeper question, why do we
lose those we do have? And we do. There is no one reading
these pages, I venture to say, who doesn't have some family member or relative who is non-practicing or has joined
another religion. Notre Dame sociologist Richard Lamanna,
for example, estimates that about one-third of the sixty million Catholics in the United States are not regular members
of a parish, and to this extent, while Catholics form the
largest religious denomination in America, non-practicing
Catholics form the second largest religious denomination in
America.

It is a sociological given that those who most lack conviction in the old faith are most likely to express an interest in the unconventional, magical, and religious doctrines. And one of the most distressing problems is precisely the cultural Catholic, the religiously illiterate, those who know so little about their own Catholic faith that they represent forty percent of those who join cults. And what would be the basis for this? Some might say teachings like *Humanae Vitae*, women's ordination issues, authority problems, sexual issues, the rise of modern science, which keeps closing the gap requiring God, all of these figure in the equation. I don't want to examine these, but to zone in on and belabor another significant and relevant finding, and here I quote sociologist Rodney Stark:

> Sometimes a traditional faith and its organized expression can become so worldly that it cannot serve the universal need for religious compensators. That is, religious bodies can become so empty of supernaturalism that they cannot serve the religious needs of the privileged either. At such moments, the privileged will seek new options.

—*The Rise of Christianity*, p. 39.

When there is no difference between the secular culture and the church culture, why should one bother with the latter? Why shouldn't people seek elsewhere where there is a difference, where the flatness of secularism gives way to the transcendent? Because, by and large, what is common to all New Agers is that they are seeking transcendent experience.

It has been observed that younger Catholics, the children of the baby boomers, do not want a religion that is merely a baptized psychology or sociology. They want a religion that purports, as it traditionally has, to place them in touch with the supernatural. They want to belong to a church filled

35

with the mystery of Christ, a church of sacraments and grace that has a message of salvation beyond the obtaining of rights and peace in this world. The same story has been tracked in mainline Protestantism, usually a bellwether in what is trendy. Roger Finks and Rodney Stark in *The Churching of America 1776-1990* show that early Protestant churches had great intensity, community, and a deep sense of the supernatural. But they gradually discarded all of this, went heavily into social and secular issues and trimmed devotions, and the result was that the more a Protestant denomination accommodated itself to the secular culture, the more some of its members became uncomfortable and the more they left or turned elsewhere leaving some mainline Protestant churches today, as we know, struggling for survival.

Sect-Like Practices

Sociologist Patricia Wittbert recounts that a good number of baby boomers are joining groups with sect-like qualities, Zen ashrams, and fundamentalist sects. She notes that Southern Baptists are going on weekend retreats and have prayer hours and meditation. The United Methodists are shifting from social justice to spirituality and have even attempted a Methodist form of monasticism. Jews are turning to medieval Jewish mysticism. (Did you know that the secular Jews, the richest, most influential, and most educated—76% of Jews attend college—constitute more than a third of Americans that have joined Hare Krishna?) The Eastern Orthodox Church is gaining converts because it is perceived "as more rooted in mystery and paradox" and over one hundred fifty Protestant congregations have converted en masse to Orthodoxy as Latinos are going en masse into Pentecostal sects.

Now all this must make us pause and ask hard questions which we will raise again in this book. Have we become so worldly, secular, and devoid of supernaturalism that Catholics have to seek meditation and spirituality elsewhere? How many Catholic converts to fundamentalism have declared that this is the first time they met Jesus Christ? How many embrace the music, the mantras, the crystals, and the artifacts of New Age because the parish has abandoned the mythical, the symbolic? These were the sensual things behind which powers lurked and wonder and folklore held sway, where beggars were saints in disguise, animals had wisdom, sky and water spoke to people, Canute held back the waves, the stag acted as a living lectern which held the Scriptures in its antlers for the holy monk to read, Jerome walked his lion, Pachome walked across the waters on crocodiles' backs, Francis preached to birds and calmed the wolf. As Malle, the madwoman in *The Man on a Donkey* sighs to her young friend, "Think of it, Wat! God in a bit of bread, come to bring morning into the darkness of our bellies!" Indeed, some things frequently slipped into superstition and abuse, but there was no doubt that all reality was interwoven with a sense of the divine. The point is that we may not agree with nor can we accept New Age's serious theological mistakes concerning grace, community, the incarnation, and the rest, but we must, once more, take it seriously. Its sense of the paranormal and what it can say to us, remind us that we have left our "First Love." The New Age, in its own counterfeit way, calls us back to it.

3. With its human-potential techniques and its use of visualization and images, the New Age has refocused public attention on the power of meditation and contemplation, a rich reality deep and profound in our own tradition, but which we have too long neglected at least at the parish level, leaving such "esoteric" things to the retreat houses and retreat masters. I'm not talking here about the meditation that some ballplayers use to "find their center" in order to make them better pitchers or outfielders, but the meditation that puts us

in touch with Mystery, the Divine. And there is no reason why Catholics cannot "baptize" certain techniques like yoga, Tai chi (rumored to ward off Alzheimer's disease), or the Enneagram and put them into the traditional Catholic context.

Widening Our Vision

4. The New Age agenda has forced us to widen our vision of revelation. Under the pressure of heresy and persecution, the early church closed revelation with the canonical books. And so, no new authoritative revelations could be added. We did not look at other more inclusive and innovative interpretations and put a period to revelation, even though at times we snuck it in through various Marian apparitions. In short, we restricted revelation to pages on a book and closed ourselves off to wider hints of God's current activity in the world and the power of intuition, emotion, and inspiration to reveal God. The New Age appropriation of eastern traditions, mantras, artifacts, crystals, and literature, on the other hand, has reminded us that we can't limit the grace of God and that even Jesus can be "the way and the truth and the life" in a pluralistic society. Thomas Merton saw this early on. Yoga, meditation, eastern techniques, the genius of other religions and traditions can be mined for their usefulness to the Catholic tradition.

New Age reminds us of our own tradition: that we don't have to search for the Spirit. Spirit is there all the time, we just have to become aware. It's the treasure in the field. Spirit, in short, is present. We are absent. We must become more present to what is already there and everything is grist for the mill. Everything is a challenge. And everything has a potential to awaken us to what is hidden, to what is behind the appearance. This is the appeal of Celtic spirituality which is often associated with New Age. It prefers John who listened to the heartbeat of the Divine over Peter who represents authority. It is creation-focused. As J. Philip Newell put it in his fine book, *Listening for the Heartbeat of God*:

> The feature of Celtic spirituality that is probably most widely recognized, both within and outside the church, is its creation emphasis... Our earliest memories are generally of wonder in relation to the elements. Do we not all carry within us, for instance, something of the memory of first listening to the waters of a river or to rainfall, or lying in the grass, feeling and smelling it and seeing its brilliant green, or watching sunlight dappling through leaves?

Connected to these moments will be recollections of experiencing at the deepest of levels a type of communion with God in nature, but there will usually have been very little in our religious traditions to encourage us to do much more than simply thank God for creation. The preconception behind this is that God is separate from creation. How many of us were taught actually to look for God within creation and to recognize the world as the place of revelation and the whole of life as sacramental? Were we not for the most part led to think that spirituality is about looking away from life, so that the church is distanced from the world and spirit is almost entirely divorced from the matter of our bodies, our lives, and the world?

"[In the Celtic prayers] the lights of the skies, the sun and moon and stars are referred to as graces, the spiritual coming through the physical and God is seen as the Life within all life and not just the Creator who set life in motion from afar" (p. 3-4). It is interesting how compatible this insight is with the current evolutionary viewpoint.

Anyway, all this says: You don't have to be a Native American to sense the sacredness of nature. You don't have to be a Buddhist to appreciate meditation. You don't have to be a Catholic to understand mysticism. You don't have to be a New Ager who is concerned with the environment and preserving the earth from pollution because of a pantheistic view of the universe that is quite incompatible with Christianity, to realize that we can copy their concern on very strong Christian theological principles. In short, we can tap into a widened vision of revelation, and the New Age has reminded us of another truth in our tradition.

5. New Age human-potential optimism has at least reminded us that the goal of Jesus was indeed transformation. The truth is that we Christians have forgotten to expect surprises and wonders of the Spirit. Not the New Agers! Their landscape is filled with angels and miracles that occur daily. But us? We expect nothing today in our lifetime. Instead we keep looking back to some kind of a golden age when angels and miracles occurred to get the religion started, but are no longer needed.

And that habit of looking back puts us out of sync with the first Christians who looked forward, forward to newness and an outpouring of the Spirit and what the Almighty would do for them in the future. "Behold, all generations shall call me blessed." A new dawn was always arriving. They were an escatological people. Even as the end of this millennium approaches, the emphasis, certainly of the fundamentalists, will be on those terrible apocryphal signs of destruction; that is to say, endings, not a new beginning, not a new age. The New Agers, however, with their insistence on human potential, remind us that we should expect transformation of ourselves and our world and, to that extent, they force us to reappropriate the message of hope.

The Fear of Death

6. The New Age doctrine of reincarnation is basically an answer to the aging baby boomers' fear of death. And an appealing answer it is. Why else would those banal after-

death and near-death books be so popular? It says that we continue on. Something more awaits us. We live on in another life. This is in sharp contrast to the old Catholic teaching which simply does not resonate with aging baby boomers struggling with mortality. What is that teaching? It is summed up in the motto, *Requiescat in pace*, rest in peace. This meant, that for one racked with pain and hurt, death is surcease, and to that extent, rest and peace at death were something to celebrate. But we have let the phrase fall into the concept of the beloved in deep freeze and the static notion that the way you die is the way you stay. We offer a Platonic heaven. You remain in your different "places" or slots in heaven, with the great saints near the upper level and most of us near the middle or towards the bottom levels, for which, nevertheless, we are grateful just to be there. And then, what do you do all day in heaven? Passivity and boredom are the images. There are only so many notes the harp can play in eternity. And what about our traditional "last things": death, judgment, heaven, and hell? They are interpreted to be static enough to be exceedingly unattractive to a people obsessed with self-improvement.

But, in fact, New Agers, with their emphasis on human potential and reincarnation, will help us recover something richer from our tradition. Doesn't death in fact mark a pivotal point in human growth—let us say boldly, a rebirth? Who is not to say that after death we continue to grow, experience, feel, and delight, that life after death is an adventure with the vast communion of saints? That there is a continuous ongoingness? And who is to say that eventually even the "damned" are saved, as their more arduous transformation takes place? Actually, we have the seeds of this concept in the teaching on Purgatory. Purgatory means a process of "purification" after death, continuous education if you will. Note, it is a process, movement, a real transformation. If New Age reincarnation strikes us as absurd and against our teaching, it nevertheless can provoke in us a better explanation and appreciation of the positive growth dynamics of death and resurrection.

The Communion of Saints

7. The high individualism of the New Age canon can force a Catholic reaction, namely, a refocus on the hidden treasure we call variously the communion of saints, the mystical body, the vine and the branches, the people of God, and so on. Faith joined to the new ecology can emphasize that indeed "we are all connected" and that spirituality, intractably reflecting the Trinity, basically lies in communion and community, and that social justice is indeed "constitutive" to the gospel message.

8. Finally, New Agers force us to take a second look at a neglected truth of Christianity, that of healing and the holistic connection between mind and body. New Agers are into it, even if they place the source within themselves. But they help us to remember that Jesus' ministry was largely a healing one. More than one-fifth of the gospel stories are devoted to Jesus' healing ministry, and forty-one instances of mental and physical healing are listed. But we ignored that in time, and we soon succumbed to Greek philosophical (and later Enlightenment) dualism and zeroed in on the soul. Our aim was to help it escape from this valley of tears. Saving disembodied souls became our interest and concern.

The net result, to be honest, is that we modern Catholics really don't expect any healing apart from the medical community. Besides, we may feel that all those biblical healing stories are symbolic anyhow and, even if they were literal, the age of healing was over once Christianity's credentials were established. We've been so successful in such attitudes that today, when people think of healing, they do not think of church, do they? They think of doctors, hospitals, clinics, and the power of positive-thinking gurus with bursts of energy. As our spirituality has declined, so has the ministry of healing, once so essential and defining for Christianity.

But it's New Age thinking that's helping us to reclaim our healing heritage. We are now very well aware that, although science has conquered, for the most part, the traditional diseases, our modern lifestyle, so far removed from the purposes of our primitive biology, has brought a sickness peculiarly its own, namely, stress. Dr. Herbert Benson, president of the Mind/Body Medical Institute of Boston's Deaconess Hospital and Harvard Medical School, says, "Anywhere from sixty to ninety percent of visits to doctors are in the mind-body stress-related realm." In this vein, consider the following:

Item: A 1995 study at Darmouth-Hitchcock Medical Center found that one of the best predictors of survival among 232 heart-surgery patients was the degree to which the patients said they drew comfort and strength from religious faith.

Item: A survey of 30 years on blood pressure showed that churchgoers have lower blood pressure than non-churchgoers.

Item: Other studies have shown that men and women who attend church regularly have half the risk of dying from coronary-artery disease as those who rarely go to church.

Item: A 1966 National Institute on Aging study of 4,000 elderly living at home in North Carolina found that those who attend religious services are less depressed and physically healthier than those who don't attend or who worship at home.

Item: Numerous studies have found lower rates of depression and anxiety-related illness among the religiously committed.

Item: Non-churchgoers are found to have a suicide rate four times higher than church regulars.

Item: A Time-Yankevich poll of 1,004 Americans conducted

in June of 1996 found that 82% believed in the healing power of prayer.

All this doesn't mean that we have to go out and advertise, "Come to church and live longer," but rather that we have to recognize that parishes have a natural propensity and context for socialization, prayer, meditation, and healing. It's a tradition that needs to be recovered. And, above all, in this day of deep alienation, we can offer community and hospitality, two crying needs. Anyway, we can dabble, as I said, in the New Age, ever conscious of its serious limitations, but also ever mindful of its potential to call us back to the rich treasures of our own tradition.

To Sum Up

The New Age phenomenon is a loose term for the eclectic borrowing of many items derived from various sources, mostly eastern religions and western humanistic psychology, all of which represent an alternative way of dealing with life beyond the traditional Judeo-Christian ways. It has serious faults and to that extent is dangerous to a healthy faith: it is thinly disguised paganism in its monism and pantheism; it has no room for grace or the incarnation; it has little social conscience and, in its individualism, has no need for church. It more than flirts with the occult and the superstitious. It is rife with new self-proclaimed and self-validating gurus selling the latest fad. It even uses Christian Scripture to seduce: Jesus answered, "Is it not written in your law, 'I said you are gods?' " (John 10:34). There, we are all divine! We must beware of its attractive literature, which at best is comforting and sentimental and at worst is theologically naive, muddle-headed, self-centered, and anti-Christian. Perhaps New Age's best judgment comes from writer Belden Lane:

> I'm increasingly uncomfortable with current images of God found in books and workshops

that mix popular psychology with a theology wholly devoted to self-realization. They seem to reverse the first question of the catechism I studied as a child, declaring that "the chief end of God is to glorify men and women, and to enjoy them forever." I really don't want a God who is solicitous of my every need, fawning for my attention, eager for nothing in the world so much as the fulfillment of my self-potential. One of the scourges of our age is that all our deities are house-broken and eminently companionable. Far from demanding anything, they ask only how they can more meaningfully enhance the lives of those they serve.

— *The Solace of Fierce Landscapes*, p. 53

On the other hand, in all this thicket of the New Age, it portrays a desire for the transcendent. To that extent, as we have just seen, it does challenge us to reconsider our own "Age Old" traditions of spirit, sacrament, mysticism, liturgy, church, and community. And if the biggest danger from the New Age is to those Catholics who do not know their own tradition and teachings, then the answer is to re-enter and re-learn our own tradition through study, books, seminars, and retreats. Likewise, the best insulation, especially for the young, is a well grounded religious education, youth ministry, and guiding adults particularly in times of transition. And that advice is especially needed as we approach the next chapter on fundamentalism.

3

Are You Saved?

The fundamentalists are funny enough, and the funniest
thing about them is their name. For, whatever else the fundamentalist is, he is not fundamental. He is content with
the bare of Scripture—the translation of a translation, coming down to him by the tradition of a tradition—without
venturing to ask for its original authority.
—G.K. Chesterton

New Age advocates look with disdain on fundamentalism
and fundamentalism returns the compliment in spades. Yet
as we shall see in chapter five, on one point, the end of the
world, they become strange bedfellows. We have focused
on New Agers in the previous chapter, but who are these
fundamentalists? Whoever they are, they are numerous.
Fundamentalists in fact abound around the world: Islamic,
Jewish, Muslim, Buddhist, Confucist, Hindu. There is no
place on the globe that doesn't harbor pockets of fundamentalists, some quietist, some aggressive, some militant,
some dangerous. In this list are included the ones we are
interested in for this chapter: North American Protestant fundamentalists. To them we must turn.

Protestant fundamentalists, like all other fundamentalists,
share one vital conviction: they are victims confronted with
the "disintegration of our social order" (Jerry Falwell). They
have become outsiders in their own society, "strangers," in

the words of one of their revivalist hymns, "within a foreign land, prisoners of a new Babylonian captivity." Why? Because the secularizing state, with its rationalized bureaucracy, has penetrated all spheres of life by introducing secular, humanistic education, prohibiting religious practices in school, and encouraging extramarital sex, homosexuality, abortion, and divorce. Fundamentalists accordingly feel that they have been marginalized by an atheistic, materialistic, anti-Christian society. They look with alarm as they see their members going over to the secular world and buying into cultural relativism, thus displacing the timeless true religion. They feel there is no choice but to form enclaves of resistance to the dominant secular way of life. They will be the Believing Remnant, the Last Outpost, the Covenant Keepers to hold the ever subversive modernity at bay. They must demonstrate the separation of the saved and the sinful. Indeed, they are aware that every day they face the three-fold enemy: a tepid or corrupt religious establishment, the secular state, and secularized civil society. And they will fight back defining fundamentalism (in the words of Marty and Appleby, who are scholars of fundamentalism), as "a religious way of being that manifests itself as a strategy by which beleaguered believers attempt to preserve their distinctive identity as a people or group."

Like the character played by Peter Finch in the movie *Network*, they cry out, "Hell, no! We're not going to take it anymore!" Marty and Appleby, in the first volume of their edited four-volume work on fundamentalism, take up this motif of "fighting" as the fundamentalist distinguishing mark. They note that fundamentalists fight back in that they are militant and reactive, whether in words or ballots or, rarely, bullets. Their core identity is perceived as threatened. Central issues are not to be negotiated, for if they lose here, they lose everything they fight for. If "secular humanism" assaults the most intimate zones of life such as the family, sex roles, the raising and education of children, they will fight for their understanding of what is right in these areas. They fight with an appeal to (highly selective) teachings of the past. They fight against all others who subvert their ways. That would be any "modernist" or compromiser of the truth. Finally, they carry out God's crusade against the forces of evil. In short, fundamentalism is a conscious organized opposition to the disruption of orthodox traditions.

Who Are They?

Fundamentalists are not conservatives—a much broader term—but basically a subdivision of them. They share with conservative Christians classic support of traditional interpretations of the Bible. Indeed, so do most Americans, with seventy-two percent saying that the Bible is the Word of God; some thirty-nine percent say it should be read literally, two-thirds believe in Jesus' resurrection, and three-fourths in life after death. And conservatism has many other subdivisions. Fundamentalists are to be found in that conservative branch called evangelicals, people who claim that only an individual acceptance of Jesus as one's personal savior and the need to "win back souls for Christ" mark the true believer. They often speak of being "born again." (What was that witticism? the trouble with born-again Christians is that they're even more of a pain the second time around!)

Where did they come from? Present-day American fundamentalism originated in the 1830s and 40s here in the United States in the period of the Great Awakening and Christian revival meetings in the south. It grew in the early 1890s and emerged stronger in the early decades of the 1900s as confidence in America's destiny began to wane in the face of labor unrest and social problems and the scientific breakthroughs that seemed to undermine Christianity. In biology, the evolutionary theory of Charles Darwin seemed to contradict the biblical accounts of creation by postulating that the earth gradually evolved over a period of millions of years, and that humans themselves have evolved from lower forms of life. In psychology, Sigmund Freud claimed that human freedom of will is an illusion, that our choices are really determined by unconscious motives and dynamisms buried deep in our psyche. In economics, Karl Marx maintained that religion is a creation of the ruling classes to control the working classes and the poor: "Don't worry if you have to suffer in this life; you will be rewarded in the life to come." In sociology, there was rapid urbanization and industrialization which displaced families and communities and there was an ominous flood of Catholic immigrants. In religion, liberal theologians were applying scientific principles to the Bible, searching for meaning within the historical context in which it was written and not worrying about literalism. Some scholars were, in the light of the discovery of rich diversity, questioning the uniqueness of Christianity and even of Christ as sole Savior, promoting religious tolerance, which to fundamentalists smacked of relativism (which is why they will have no part in ecumenism). After all, if Jesus was not a virgin-born miracle worker who rose from the dead, he was history's worst hoax. If he wasn't coming back again soon, where was hope? If the Bible is unreliable, where is salvation to be found?

Fundamentalist response to all these assaults on traditional religion was very diversified and its followers quarreled furiously among themselves over the biblical texts and the new science. But between the years 1910 and 1915, in reaction to the liberal Protestant biblical studies, some conservative Protestant scholars, greatly abetted by some professors at Princeton, wrote a series of booklets called *The Fundamentals*. In the series they rejected the "modernist" attempt to accommodate Christian teaching to the claims of science. They insisted on strict adherence to a number of doctrinal points, with five main "fundamental" ones:

1. the absolute inspiration and inerrancy of the words of the Bible;

2. the virginal birth and divinity of Jesus Christ;

3. the substitutionary atonement for our sins through Christ's death on the cross;

4. the bodily resurrection of Christ;

5. the literal Second Coming of Christ at the end of time.

They felt secure in knowing that this basic agenda would set things right. American Protestantism was always so full of optimism anyway. In this new Promised Land of America, Protestants were meant to triumph. Which is why, at the end of the nineteenth century they boldly named one of their prestigious magazines *The Christian Century*, for indeed they believed that a new wave of Christianity would sweep the twentieth century. Victory after victory would roll on. They were confident and numerous, prompting H.L. Mencken to scoff that if he heaved an egg out of a Pullman window anywhere in the country he would hit a fundamentalist, whom he characterized as ignorant country bumpkins. But shortly after Mencken's words, a traumatic event happened for fundamentalists, namely, the famous "Monkey Trial" in 1925 where the issue was the teaching of Darwinian evolution by a high school teacher, Thomas Scopes. The world watched Clarence Darrow and William Jennings Bryan fight it out, and in the end, the fundamentalists were left heaped with ridicule and their reputation in tatters. In the 1930s and 40s they slipped underground. This well-publicized episode made them realize more and more that they were, and must be, out of step with the culture. From this point on they knew that they could not be part of the

American mainstream anymore, that they were different.

But, far from disappearing, they went about quietly building an infrastructure. And, far from rejecting all aspects of modernity, they took full advantage of television and transportation and marketing techniques. They went on to found churches, radio stations, clinics, publishing houses, foreign mission societies, Bible Institutes, like the Moody Institute and Wheaton Institute in Chicago, and the Inter-Varsity Fellowship, the Youth for Christ movement, and Campus Crusade for Christ on college campuses. Radio especially was their entrance into American homes and the key to their revival. Radio preachers like Paul Rader and Charles Fuller helped overcome Mencken's cruel description of them. When people were turning to religion in the anxious days of World War II, the fundamentalists were there and one of their radio preachers became so famous he even made fundamentalism respectable: Billy Graham.

But also, we should note, there was simultaneously a momentous though subtle change in strategy during this time. They moved from the position, dominant from the Monkey Trial to the 60s, that the world was sinking deeper and deeper into moral chaos and sin and would do so until Jesus returned and founded the kingdom of the righteous and therefore the world must be renounced (called pre-millennialism). They moved from this stance to the conviction that no, Jesus would come only after faithful Bible-believing Christians had prepared the way by inaugurating the era of righteousness (called post-millennialism). In other words, they could no longer wait around passively for the rot to collapse and Jesus to come. They themselves had to actively prepare the way for Jesus. Thus was born, in the wake of the moral and social crisis of the 60s, the activist, lobbying fundamentalists, the "new morality," Jerry Falwell's Moral Majority, Pat Robertson's Christian Coalition of the late 1980s, and the Christian Right, all designed to have a national impact on politics and to influence (which they did) such presidents as Ronald Reagan and George Bush.

Catholic Fundamentalism

Meanwhile, before we proceed further with our look at Protestant fundamentalism, we should pause to take note of Catholic fundamentalism, which was happening at the same time. These were and are the post-Vatican II Catholics who are dismayed at some of the sweeping changes of that council, a sweep which disposed of many good things including its defining identity. Such Catholics are characterized by an unquestioning loyalty to Rome (in contrast to the liberal Catholic's ongoing public criticism and dissension), a veneration of Mary and the saints (in contrast to "the stripping of the altars" in modern churches), clerical authoritarianism (in contrast to do-it-yourself cafeteria Catholicism), and a consciousness of sin (in contrast to the culture's adoption of the therapeutic). Be it noted that most fundamentalist Catholics do not disown Vatican II, however much they might secretly detest it and wish it had never happened, because they are caught in the bind of professing loyalty to the magisterium and consequently the need to accept the magisterium's council. So while they do not openly contest the council, they vehemently decry the liberal interpretation of it. In fact, one of their academic enterprises is to go back to the council documents to proclaim "what they really say."

What bothers them is frustration and moral outrage that the church has basically abandoned its tradition and instead adopted the culture's secular norms and deconstructions. What bothers them is the spiritual, cultural, and moral chaos in Catholicism since the council. There's no definition, no identity, no center, no authority to Catholicism anymore. It's Protestantism all over again with its endless divisions and factions. They have nothing to hand down to their children or grandchildren who have stopped attending Mass. They are put off as they see Catholicism becoming more modern-ized and rationalized. They see its rich devotional life dis-appearing and find the church less mysterious and enchant-ing than before. They see the virgin birth, the resurrection, heaven and hell all reduced to metaphors. They see the the-ologians and their liberal agendas replacing the magisterium, forging an American church largely independent of Vatican control.

They witness parish priests openly defying *Humanae Vitae* (a linchpin of dissent for the liberals and of loyalty for the conservatives). They see nuns abandoning religious life in large numbers and adopting the tenets of American fem-inism. They see any norms regulating sex abandoned to what they would call the "MTV clerical crowd." After all, what are they to make of the liberal statement of the American Catholic Theological Commission that "A homo-sexual engaging in homosexual acts in good conscience has the same rights of conscience and the same right to the sacraments as a married couple practicing birth control in good conscience?" Substitute their fifteen-year-old son or daughter for "homosexual" in that sentence and they are repulsed at this norm which they perceive is no norm at all but license.

Fundamentalist Catholics are also quite perplexed at the Vatican II documents on religious liberty and ecumenism, which state that all people must be free to practice the reli-gion of their choice, for indeed other religions have value. But to them, this flatly contradicts a steady tradition found in scores of encyclicals, which categorically affirms that the Catholic church alone possesses all truth and is the certain means of salvation. Loyal Catholics hold true to the tradition. The council therefore is in schism because it broke with tra-dition. They are positively livid at the bishops for their tepid approach to abortion, their lack of front-line witness and financial support. In a church which has sold out to the secular culture, which has become morally anemic, and for which martyrdom is considered pathological, they hold that taking a stand on abortion becomes a kind of last chance to testify to the transcendent and to commitment. Above all, they decry what has happened to the liturgy with its new anthropocentric emphasis—with all the mystery and cadence gone. They say the Mass has been robbed of its awesome texture and tone and turned into a banal feel-good gathering with no challenges beyond the psychological well-being of the participants. They are distraught with the U.S. bishops for their cowardice in standing up to the church-destroying liberals and even angrier with Pope John Paul II for going through the motions of retrenchment, but not being bold enough to throw the liberals out of the church.

Becoming Separatists

Some decided to act. From the 60s on, some fundamentalist Catholics, citing ironically the council's own declaration of the laity's privileges, have become separatists creating their own communities. In this they stand in a firm American tradition of the many utopian communities that have dotted the landscape ever since the country was founded. Currently, in fact, there are over three hundred traditionalist communities across the United States. Early on, Gommar De Pauw from Mt. St. Mary's in Emmitsburg, Maryland, founded the Catholic Traditionalist Movement, dedicated to slowing down the radical changes in the liturgy and keeping the Tridentine Mass alive. Bishop Marcel Lefebvre came along and established the priestly fraternity of the Society of St. Pius X to ordain priests in the old tradition. The Society has its own seminary and press (Angelus Press) in Winona, Minnesota and its headquarters in Kansas City.

Then there is the Society of St. Pius V, more radical than Lefebvre's group from which it broke off. There is also the Tridentine Latin Rite church at Mount St. Michael's near

Spokane, Washington, which, under its founder, Father Francis Schuckardt, turned out to be a sadistic enclave of sexual and physical abuse by him. Father Schuckardt was forced to flee to northern California where he and eleven of his followers were subsequently arrested on drug possession, stolen property, and illegal weapons charges. He is now in the Pacific northwest calling his group Oblates of Mary Immaculate. Meanwhile, in spite of the scandals of its founder, Mt. St. Michael is flourishing and continues and revolves around the belief that the popes who presided over the Vatican Council were in fact heretical popes, anti-popes, and therefore in reality the see of Peter is and remains vacant.

Guidance from Apparitions

Other fundamentalist Catholics seek salvation and guidance from the Marian apparitions, some of which, in imitation of the Protestant millennial groups we shall see in chapter five, are in the apocalyptic endtime mode. Others are consistently intrigued by the "Fatima secret" and are greatly annoyed that the pope and the bishops have not consecrated Russia to the Immaculate Heart of Mary as she ordered. For this reason and others, some have gone so far as to declare that Pope John Paul II is a false pope, a captive of communist forces intent on the infiltration of the church. Just as others have declared Pope John XXIII and Pope Paul VI, especially after the latter promulgated the New Order of the Mass, not as the anti-popes of the Mt. St. Michael crowd, but as outright impostors, communist spies bent on destroying the church. After all, could a real pope change the Mass that way? Paul VI must have been an imposter.

In fact, on August 6, 1993, the Blessed Virgin told Veronica Leuken (of the Bayside, Queens apparitions) that the imposter was a professional actor who had been surgically remade into Paul VI. The Virgin's exact words: "Plastic surgery, my child, the best of surgeons were used to create this imposter. Shout it from the rooftops!" There's more: some fundamentalist Catholics hold that after the deaths of Pius XII and Pope John XXIII, Cardinal Giuseppe Siri, a conservative from Genoa, was really elected pope, but his election was suppressed by threats from the worldwide Judeo-Masonic forces bent on destroying the church and kept from the public and he, the real pope, was sent into exile (something like Dumas' classic, *The Man in the Iron Mask*). Conspiracy theories abound among the more rabid fundamentalists.

To find Catholic fundamentalists, click on the TV to Mother Angelica's enormously popular and well funded Eternal Word Network (EWTN), and you'll find a stained-glass background, a book stand to the left, and a monk attired in full habit sitting in a chair facing the camera. No music or choir here. He talks to the viewers about the decline of values in American life and the increase in sexual promiscuity. His message today is especially for Catholics: "The vocation of a Catholic is to be obedient to Holy Mother Church," he implores. His logic is that the pope, as successor to St. Peter, and the Catholic hierarchy are entrusted with the truth of Jesus Christ. If U.S. Catholics would obey official church teachings they would be a leaven, an effective influence on the rest of the culture.

He quotes the Bible and Catholic doctrine regarding sexual norms. His voice rises and he becomes flushed, saying: "Catholic theologians, and yes, some parish priests, are confusing the faithful with theological speculation. They interpret doctrine according to their own opinion and on their own terms." He outlines his argument in a twenty-minute sermon, then punctuates his closing remarks with a muted slam of his fist on the podium, speaking forcefully: "The Ten Commandments are not the 'Ten Suggestions,' and the Catholic church is not a democracy! The holy father does not take opinion polls to make up his mind. Be faithful to the holy father or leave the church. There is no room for 'cafeteria Catholics,' who pick and choose what they want to believe." A small paperback book on sexual morality is offered by an announcer at the end of the show along with an address and an 800 number.

The speaker is but reflecting other fundamentalist Catholics such as Catholics United for the Faith (CUF), Opus Dei, The Blue Army, and Bishop Marcel Lefebvre's group. Common to these television shows, Protestant and Catholic, is an underlying outlook on life and religion, namely, antagonism to modern culture, watered-down religion, and secular humanism. In this context it is worth emphasizing here that many mainstream Catholics, and not just separatists or traditionalist Catholics, reject some of Vatican II's sweeping reforms and have misgivings about them. Many mainliners are perplexed and unhappy with their church which seems all out of kilter, so unfocused, in these post-Vatican II days. Perhaps that is why Dominican Thomas O'Meara estimates that twenty percent of the revenues of Oral Roberts, Pat Robertson, and Jimmy Swaggert come from Catholics. Likewise, he notes, thousands of Catholics have joined fundamentalist prayer groups and flock to their preaching and healing services.

At the Grass-Roots Level

But enough of the political and social background of fundamentalism. From here on in, we want to focus on fundamentalists where we ourselves are likely to meet them: fervent evangelicals living at the grass-roots level as our salespeople, neighbors, friends, and even, painfully for some, our family members. And, in a most practical and pastoral way, we want to see how they evangelize us and how to respond to them. First of all, we must take note that five features identify them since these features will be present when they talk to us.

1. The first is evangelism. If there is one thing they know it is that they are saved. If you are not saved, you'd better be, for being "saved" is the sure way to heaven. It is therefore incumbent upon them, the "saved," to bring Jesus to you, the unsaved. Hence evangelism, their strong proselytizing.

2. Second, there is inerrancy: the Bible in their eyes contains no mistakes. No part of it can be in error; if but one error of fact or principle is admitted in Scripture, then nothing is certain, even the redemptive work of Christ. True Christians must take the whole Bible, even the parts they don't like. The Bible will provide an accurate description of science, history, morality, and religion (although they really do some fancy footwork here in that they do not question some aspects of science, such as the world is round or goes around the sun, while other biblical descriptions such as the "waters" in the creation story which are above and below the earth are said to be "poetic," and teachings condoning slavery or polygamy are neutralized as irrelevant to salvation. Actually, the leaders argue a lot over biblical interpretations but this rarely reaches the rank and file). This gives them the sense, as Kathleen Boone has pointed out, of imagining themselves "either steadfast in absolute truth or whirling in the vortex of nihilism."

3. The third is what is called "dispensational pre-millennialism." This means that salvation will be "dispensed" to the Christian faithful at the Coming of Christ prior to the millennium, the 1000-year reign of Christ. They look forward to the rapture or "the snatch," in which all the Christian faithful, at the end of the world, will disappear in an instant as they rise to heaven with Christ. Hence the bumper sticker, "This car will be unoccupied at the rapture." Everyone else will be fried.

4. Fourth, there is separatism. There are to be no dissent-

ing opinions. There must be uniformity of belief and practice. They are therefore independent of mainline Protestant churches which they consider corrupt or tepid. There is no room for backsliding, no room, as we said before, for ecumenical relations with other churches. The truth can be found only within fundamentalism. There must not only be uniformity of faith but separation from those whose beliefs and practices are suspect. Moral discipline and the reinforcements of the community maintain such a separatism. In other words, fundamentalists, wary of assimilation into the secular culture, form an enclave of protection and assault.

They grieve over members who have succumbed to the alluring culture, one that promises instant gratification and rewards. They themselves are the "remnant," the ones who remain faithful, the "saved," the "saints." Beware of infiltrators. They're everywhere. And this suspicion is the basis of a growing conspiracy theory which we will discuss in the next chapter. To get you into their protective community is their goal.

Charismatic Leaders

5. Finally, there is the charismatic leader. To keep their agenda intact, fundamentalists stress the importance of authority within their congregations to enforce conformity, strict norms, and consensus. That is why the typical form of fundamentalist organization is charismatic, a leader-follower relationship. (It is always profitable to remember, as we shall mention again, that although Catholicism has the public image of strict central authority, evangelical conservatives, with their "infallible" ministers and firm control, would make Pius IX envious. Modern secular politically correct vigilante squads fit the same fundamentalist mold).

We might also add: the number of evangelical fundamentalists is impressive. Estimates of their numbers range from two hundred fifty million to four hundred million, giving them something like fifteen to twenty percent of the global Christian market. There can be no question that here in America their numbers and influence are pre-eminent, affecting, as we have seen, public opinion in politics and social ethics. Evangelicals have pioneered the use of television, radio, and other media to target potential converts. They have translated the Bible into hundreds of different languages and poured money and resources into their missionary efforts. There is no corner of the globe that is untouched by evangelicalism. They have captured so-called Catholic countries like Guatemala and Brazil. Southern Baptists have increased from around ten million in 1960 to fifteen million in 1990; Pentecostal denominations from under two million in 1960 to almost ten million in 1990.

Seventh Day Adventist world membership has multiplied ten times in five decades. Since 1965 the Jehovah's Witnesses in this country have grown to almost seven hundred thousand. More than fifty million Americans claim to have been born again. Indeed, impressive numbers. Yet we should also note that at the same time evangelicals have shown themselves to be quite prone to rather persistent and damaging schisms. While their numbers are indeed impressive, we must remember that the figure has to be divided among over fourteen thousand different churches and denominations. Moreover, they are deeply sectarian, with the term "church" often meaning little more than a collection of people who are presently in agreement with one another. When an ecclesial or doctrinal argument brews and no resolution is reached, all too frequently a new denomination is born.

For fundamentalists do disagree on many points and it shows in the political maneuverings and firings and witch hunting that go on. Seminaries and Bible colleges, as you often read in the papers, are regularly purged and pastors subjected to intense questioning on the orthodoxy of their beliefs. (I am always amazed, by the way, of how vocal and knowledgeable Catholics are about accusations of authoritarianism and witch-hunting in their own church and totally unaware that the same thing goes on in other denominations.) Anyway, the result is that fundamentalist evangelical churches include a broad spectrum. There are the "Assemblies of God" (the largest), the "Church of Christ of [Boston, Milwaukee, and so on]," Anabaptists; churches like the Mennonites and Baptists, Pentecostal, "Full Gospel" churches, and many others with names such as "Church of the Good Shepherd," or "Calvary Temple," Inter-Varsity, Campus Crusade, the Navigators. They may differ among themselves in some respects, but all hold to the five "fundamentals" already mentioned.

The Appeal of Fundamentalism

This is the fact: fundamentalist churches are the fastest-growing churches in America today, even though overall membership is not large. The questions naturally come to mind: What is their appeal? And why are so many Catholics seemingly attracted to them? A good understanding of the first question will enable us to answer the second and to formulate some helpful pastoral responses to the fundamentalist challenge.

In general, the appeal of fundamentalism lies, first of all, in its simplicity. Many Catholics today are confused by the differences of opinion and practice among theologians, bishops, pastors, religious, communities, parishes, and so on. The Jesus Seminar, whose chief spokesman is ex-Catholic priest Dominic Crossan, says that the New Testament is mostly myth. The late Raymond Brown, a Catholic priest, disagreed. *The National Catholic Reporter* and *The Wanderer*, both Catholic papers, disagree on almost everything. Some Catholics believe in the real presence, others say it is symbolic: one parish will bury a divorced person, another won't. The Catholic church is famous these days for its factions, its "culture wars." Call to Action, the Rutherford Institute, Catholics for Free Choice, Catholics for Contraception, women celebrating a pseudo-eucharist, Rome silencing theologians, liberal parishes, conservative parishes, the public acrimony and open name-calling, scandals—all present a spectacle of high division in the Catholic church which can't, it seems, agree on anything—even the number of holy days! It is difficult at times to know who or what to believe.

In place of all this confusion, fundamentalist preachers and believers present an appealingly simple message that promises certainty of salvation. And that is a large appeal. It is reminiscent of the terrible fourth-century arguments over the Trinity with counter excommunications, warrior monks slaying the opposition, and terms like filioque, circuminsession, Monophyitism, docetism, and a hundred other "isms" being tossed around—until out of the East in the sixth century came a man who cut through it all. His cry: "There is only one God and Allah is his name and Mohammed is his prophet." Period. Simple, basic, clear. Case closed. So with the fundamentalists. What they offer is simple. They are clear about what they believe. Nor are they the stereotype of the poor, unlettered rube. They are intelligent and have their noted scholars. They put their confidence not in any human person or organization, but in the authority of the Bible. The Word of God is their sole rule of faith, and it is to be taken literally. The Bible teaches clearly that human beings are sinners, utterly incapable of saving themselves or gaining eternal life by their own efforts.

So they give an appealingly simple explanation: our situation, they say, would be hopeless unless God intervened. But the good news is God did! God mercifully sent Jesus into the world to die for our sins. Because Jesus was both divine and human, his death had infinite value and power to wash away all our sins once and for all. But in order for this salvation to touch us personally, there is one (and only one) thing we have to do: confess our sinfulness and helplessness and invite Jesus Christ into our hearts as our personal Savior. This is not accomplished through some external ritual such as baptism (and certainly not infant baptism). Rather, it must be a personal decision arising out of a conviction of one's utter need for a Savior. And once we have made that act of surrender, we have an absolute certainty of salvation. Even our subsequent sins cannot invalidate that basic decision, so long as we continue to believe in the power of Christ to save us.

It is easy to understand that fundamentalists find profound peace and liberation in such a belief system. Whatever doubts they may have about the future of the economy, or their health, or the condition of the world, they have absolute certainty about the one thing that matters: their eternal salvation. They know they are going to heaven. This is why fundamentalists are genuinely puzzled when they ask a Catholic, "Are you saved?" and the Catholic answers, "Well, I think so. I hope so." To the fundamentalist, that waffling sounds like doubt about the saving action of Jesus Christ. (More on this later.)

Family Values

Second, another appealing aspect of fundamentalism is that its members generally appear to embody traditional and family-oriented values. In these days of a fifty percent divorce rate, broken families, a third of America's babies born out of wedlock, it's no small thing. To shore up family life, for example, the Southern Baptists, meeting in Salt Lake City in June of '98, added to their basic statement a declaration that "a wife is to submit herself graciously to her husband," bringing, of course, an outcry from liberal Protestants and snickers from feminists. No matter. The

Southern Baptists declare that the differing roles are firmly rooted in the Bible, God's blueprint for the family, which needs all the help it can get.

Third, fundamentalists are surely different. You know where they stand. They have no identity crisis—as Catholics do. Unlike mainline Christians, Methodists, Lutherans, Presbyterians, and Catholics, they are very visible and make no bones about it. The mainline Christians keep it to themselves. They don't want to intrude. Besides, religion is a private affair. You could know close friends for years and not know their religious denomination. Not so with the fundamentalists. You go to their services or watch them on TV and what you get are elaborate sets, fabulous clothes, fantastic hair styles, a long two-hour sermon, extravagance, lots of tears, and the promise of financial success. They're different. Catholics, on the other hand, are not distinguishable from the general public, according to Gallup, in anything, including divorce. Except abortion: Catholic women get more abortions than Protestant women.

Fourth, many fundamentalist believers project a positive, cheerful attitude toward life. They are warm and friendly, often the first ones to offer help in time of need. On college campuses, fundamentalist students are clean-cut and outgoing, have high moral standards, and still know how to have a good time. If you are a stranger at their church services or social gatherings, you will be warmly welcomed, introduced to everyone, and made to feel at home. For many Catholics, this is in sharp contrast to what they have experienced in the large impersonal settings of their own parish churches.

Finally, fundamentalists are, as we noted before, encouraged and trained to be evangelizers. They consider it their mission to go out and save others for Christ. Many Catholics, of course, resent it when fundamentalists persist in asking them questions like "Do you know the Lord?" or "Are you a born-again Christian?" Some Catholics consider this relentless questioning to be a form of badgering or harassing. Still, it is hard not to admire that kind of zeal and courage or to wonder why it is not more common in the Catholic church. Moreover, fundamentalists are truly committed, active, serious about their faith and the young, as always, are attracted by commitment, which may explain why so many Catholics become fundamentalists.

On the Downside

Along with the appeal of fundamentalism, however, there are some downsides, downsides that many Catholics perceive only after they have become involved in a fundamentalist church. One form it takes is a certain arrogance or smugness. Fundamentalists are not only certain of their own salvation, they have little hope for anyone else's. If you do not believe as they do, you cannot be saved. Moslems, Jews, Hindus, Catholics—they are all going to hell and they waste their time doing good deeds, for their deeds are futile. In fact, statistically, the vast majority of humankind is damned (although after the more positive Moral Majority movement in 1979, Tim LaHaye did some quick fancy computations to prove that most Americans are not in fact lost but rather are silent believers or unwitting hostages to the devious secular forces. Something like the Catholic "baptism of desire"). For some curious reason, fundamentalists seem especially anxious to convert Catholics. Perhaps they perceive us as the most deceived and blinded of all Christians, in critical danger of losing our souls. Perhaps it is because we are more clear in our doctrine than the Protestants, or we present a more defined target, or we are considered the most lost, the most perverse, or perhaps it's just the traditional bias of anti-Catholicism that is never too far below the surface.

I mean, Jimmy Swaggert made no bones about Catholic deviation. In his "Letter to My Catholic Friends," written in Baton Rouge in 1986, he writes:

Every sacrament, every good work is opposed to the salvation offered by Jesus. Catholicism, like Judaism, is not a religion of faith in Jesus but a religion of lies. Tragically, Swaggert continued, it is for this reason that millions of Catholics will die unsaved because they have been led to believe that through the work of belonging to the Catholic church and participating in the sacraments, which are nowhere mentioned in God's Word, they are accepting Jesus Christ and are thereby saved.

I have a recent advertisement from our local paper in front of me. There, in full boldface print, are the words, "Attention Catholics." Then comes the invitation to attend a lecture-video entitled "Catholicism: A Crisis of Faith" and the subtext says, "This video compares the teachings of the Catholic Church with the Bible, and includes testimonies from former priests and nuns." You can't do better than that. At any rate, fundamentalist criticisms of Catholic beliefs follow a standard summation:

1. We do not know the Bible or use it as our norm of faith.

2. We do not accept Jesus Christ as our only Savior.

3. We put our faith in Mary and the saints, sacraments, rituals, prayers, and the pope.

4. We trust more in our own works than in the cross of Christ to save us.

Separatism and Elitism

Another downside of fundamentalism is its separatism and elitism. Its literature often proclaims that "we do not have fellowship with unbelievers." "Unbelievers" apparently means anyone who does not believe in their brand of Christianity. That is why most fundamentalist churches will not work ecumenically with "mainline" Protestant and Catholic churches. Presumably, to do so would be to risk cooperating in the works of Satan. It is this kind of extremist thinking—that often spills over into extreme politics, separatist movements, dangerous sects, racism, and prejudice—that often turns away Catholics who have felt some initial attraction to a fundamentalist church.

Finally, there is a strange irony in the fundamentalist belief system that produces tensions. On the one hand, it claims that God's word in the Bible is its sole authority. Any kind of human authority or hierarchy is contrary to the mind of Christ. Yet when someone begins to question one of the fundamentalist teachings or interpretations of Scripture, he or she is promptly warned about the danger of wandering into the camp of Satan. And if the member dares to leave a fundamentalist church, the member is made to feel that he or she has chosen the path to hell. There are numerous stories about people who have experienced severe guilt feelings after leaving a fundamentalist church. There is even a support group called "Fundamentalists Anonymous" to help people deal with the internal stress and external harassment they encounter when they leave. This kind of heavy-handed authoritarianism is another negative side of fundamentalism.

4

The Bible at the Center

Yet even this to Heaven is less offense
And more endurable than when Holy Writ
Is cast aside and wrested from its sense
—Dante, *Paradiso* Canto 29

Here they are, at your door waving the Bible. Or there they are on the television waving the Bible. Or there they are sitting next to you on the plane reading the Bible. To say fundamentalists are Bible-centered is to understate a known reality. So, let's look at this Bible-centeredness of theirs, setting the stage with a quotation from Nancy Ammerman:

> Because this idea of inerrancy is so central to the identity of fundamentalists, it is an idea that receives considerable attention and development. Theologians and church leaders worry about all the nuances of interpretation and arrive at various theories that seem best to support the Bible's truthfulness. They often argue vociferously among themselves, but their worrying rarely affects the people in the pews. The primary affirmation of ordinary believers is simply that the Bible is a reliable guide for life. It contains systematic rules for living that have been proven successful over six thousand years of human history. Fundamentalists are confident

that everything in Scripture is true, and if they have questions about a seemingly difficult passage, they know that prayer, study, and a visit with the pastor are guaranteed to provide an answer.

—*Fundamentalisms Observed* "North American Protestant Fundamentalism," pp. 5-6

All this is verified on the street level. And here in this chapter, I will be interspersing some short paragraphs from Father Martin Pable's excellent little book, *Catholics and Fundamentalists* (available from Hi Time, Milwaukee, WI). He notes that in the book *Evangelicalism: The Coming Generation*, James Hunter quotes a college student as saying, "If the Bible isn't true, everything in my life would be so tentative. I think there would be no rock to go back to. Why hold so tightly to my faith if it is not even stable?" Furthermore, not only is the Bible a true and stable source of truth but it is also easy to understand, according to fundamentalists. They are fond of quoting one of their own scholars, Charles Hodge: "The Bible is a plain book. It is intelligible by the people. And they have the right and are bound to read and interpret it for themselves; so that their faith may rest on the testimony of the Scriptures, and not that of the church."

Again, that "plain" book does not have to be interpreted by experts or authorities; it can be understood by "plain" people if they read it plainly—that is, literally. All that is required is that it be read with faith and with prayer for the guidance of the Holy Spirit. That "plainness" motif undoes them. When they make statements like this, you would think they would learn from history. That was precisely the downfall of first Protestantism at the Reformation: *Scriptura Sola*, "Scripture alone" with the claim that the truth was obvious and plain for all. That is, until Luther and Melanchthon and

Zwingli read the same lines in the Bible on the eucharist, had radically differing interpretations and split off from one another. Protestants have been splitting off ever since, precisely over the question of interpreting "plain" Scripture. It is not without merit, therefore, to notice that ever since the Reformation, over twenty-five thousand different Protestant denominations have come into existence and, it is estimated, almost five new ones are being formed every day.

Ironically, we simply can't demonstrate that plain "Scripture alone" theory in Scripture itself. Nowhere does the Bible declare that it's the only and sole authority of the faith. On the contrary, in 1 Timothy 3:15, Paul writes that the church is "the pillar and foundation of truth." To back that up in a practical way, we must recall that historically the decision of what books went into the Bible was itself the product of that church, a result of a meeting of Catholic bishops at the Councils of Hippo and Carthage in the fourth century. We have to remember that some books were in contention: some thought that early works like the Epistle of Barnabas and the Acts of Paul should be included; others that Second Peter and Revelation should be excluded. Who decided but the church—those Catholic bishops meeting in councils—what went in and what stayed out? So, ironically, from the Protestant point of view, you wind up with an "infallible" book from a "fallible" source. Doesn't sound right. Then you also have the question as to how did people get saved for four hundred years before there was a canonical or official Bible?

Again, to belabor the point, there was no gospel, for instance, until about three decades after the resurrection, and even then, as Luke clearly states, his material was handed on to him "by eye-witnesses and servants of the word" (Luke 1:2)—in other words, the church; and John states forthrightly that not everything was written down: "But there are also many other things that Jesus did; if every one of them were written down, I suppose that the world itself could not contain all the books that would have been written" (John 21:24). In any case, the Catholic position is that since the Bible grew out of the church's many generational discernment, the believing community, it must still be read within that same believing community. Which is to say, we must read it within the context of church tradition. That is the location of authority, and it is precisely, by the way, the issue of authority that has caused many well-publicized converts to Catholicism by evangelical ministers because they saw fellow ministers who proclaimed the "plain" Bible give differing interpretations. There is no "referee" to decide among them. So they turned to Rome. (See, for example, Mark Shea's *By What Authority?*) The authority question is what is called in their circles "the evangelical dilemma." How can sincere, devout, Bible-reading people come to different conclusions on substantial key issues by following the Bible alone?

If the Bible is so plain, how can there be disagreement? Even more: why do fundamentalists continue to disagree among themselves to this day? And, furthermore, why don't they accept your interpretation for the meaning since you may properly claim that the biblical words are plain to you? Why don't they respect that instead of consigning you to Satan for your misreading? It soon becomes obvious, of course, that one runs into all sorts of problems when one begins to read the Bible literally—that is, without trying to interpret its meaning. For example, what does the Book of Genesis mean when it says that God created the heavens and the earth in six days (see Genesis 1)? Or what does Jesus mean when he says, "From the days of John the Baptist until now the kingdom of heaven has suffered violence, and the violent take it by force" (Matthew 11:12)? Not only are some passages in the Bible very obscure but there are also outright contradictions in some of the texts. Matthew's account of the beatitudes says that Jesus went up the mountain, gathered his disciples around him, and taught them at length, beginning with eight beatitudes (see Matthew 5:1). In Luke 6:17, we read that Jesus came down with them and stood on a level place and taught the crowd, beginning with four beatitudes. Which account is true? Was it a "Sermon on the Mount" or a "Sermon on the Plain"? Were there eight beatitudes or four?

And what about the famous passage in which Jesus tells the disciples, "And call no one your father on earth, for you have one Father—the one in heaven" (Matthew 23:9)? Fundamentalists like to quote that passage when criticizing Catholics, who address their priests as "Father." Yet, if you take a look, it is clear from later New Testament writings that early Christians continued to call their parents "father" and "mother." The first letter of John chapter 2, verse 13 says, "I am writing to you, fathers, because you know him who is from the beginning." And Paul writes, "For though you might have ten thousand guardians in Christ, you do not have many fathers. Indeed, in Christ Jesus I became your father through the gospel" (1 Corinthians 4:15). So even Paul calls himself "father." Either the inspired writers were being disobedient to Christ, or the Holy Spirit was contradicting itself—which is unthinkable—or Christ's words have to be understood in a way other than literally. Then, too, why do fundamentalists read the words of the Bible so literally, but when it comes to the famous eucharistic passage in the sixth chapter of John ("unless you eat the flesh of the Son of man and drink his blood you have no life in you…This is the bread which came down from heaven…"), they read it symbolically?

And, as everyone knows, fundamentalists have much trouble with Mary. Yet, if you ask them, do you believe the Scripture is inspired by the Holy Spirit, they answer yes. If you ask them if they believe in prophecy, they answer yes.

Then how do they contend with the Scripture passage that says that Mary, under the inspiration of the Holy Spirit, cried out, "My soul magnifies the Lord and my spirit rejoices in God my savior for he has looked with favor on the lowliness of his handmaid. Surely, from now on, all generations shall call me blessed"? Quite a prophecy. Do they call her blessed? Why not? We could go on: if the words of the Bible are to be taken plainly and literally, why don't fundamentalists wash one another's feet or invite the poor, the lame, and the blind to their lunches and dinners—since this is plainly what Jesus asks of his disciples (see John 13:14; Luke 14:12–13)?

The point is, the Bible is not as plain and simple as the fundamentalists would like to believe. As a matter of fact, when they are pressed, they will admit that the Bible needs to be interpreted. Otherwise, it's like God leaving us the Constitution of the United States with no Supreme Court to interpret it. Catholicism falls back on tradition and the magisterium as its "Supreme Court." But fundamentalists, who reject both tradition and the magisterium wholeheartedly, actually do an end-run to the same conclusion, although they can't admit it. By that I mean that their scholars have worked to produce lengthy "commentaries" on the biblical books. Why would they do that if all is so plain? One of the most popular of these today is the *Liberty Commentary on the New Testament*, edited by Jerry Falwell. Even more influential is the famous *Schofield Reference Bible*, written by C.L. Schofield, and its updated version, *The New Schofield Reference Bible*. The purpose of the commentaries is clearly to help the Christian understand the true meaning of the Bible. So you have a contradiction. On the one hand, fundamentalists claim that the devout reader can understand the text with the help of the Holy Spirit; on the other hand, they recognize the danger of every reader interpreting the text in his or her own way, which would result in biblical anarchy, so they turn to somebody's else's interpretation.

Not Widely Circulated

But you should know this open secret: these commentaries are not widely circulated among the general membership of fundamentalist Christians. They are used mainly by the pastors and preachers. Moreover, there is often disagreement among the commentators themselves. For example, the book of Revelation describes a vision of two hundred million horses and riders bringing plagues to the earth (Revelation 9:13–19). The horses have a fantastic appearance, tails like snakes and heads like those of lions breathing out fire, smoke, and sulphur. They are sent to destroy one-third of the human race. Now, how is this vision to be interpreted? One fundamentalist commentator, Oliver Greene, says that the horses must be understood as some kind of supernatural beings. On the other hand, Leon Bates calls them "vehicles" that kill by fire, smoke, and "projectiles"; hence, they may be the equivalent of modern missile-launching tanks. And finally, Hal Lindsey claims the passage is a prophecy of modern nuclear war.

A lady from Red Bank, New Jersey, Betty Wulf, the lady of four husbands who changed her name to Claire Prophet, spiritual leader of the Church Universal and Triumphant out in Montana, read the book of Revelation and predicted that there would be a Nuclear Holocaust in March of 1990. March 1990 has come and gone and her sect is now declining. Chen Hon-Ming predicted that God was to appear on television on channel 18 on March 25th, 1998, and then descend to the backyard of 3513 Ridgeland Way, Garland, Texas. One hundred and fifty Taiwanese of God's Salvation Church showed up. God didn't. The Heaven's Gate disaster folk in San Diego read the Bible to come up with their sick scenario. The Jehovah's Witnesses, as we shall note again in the next chapter, have routinely predicted for almost a century the coming of Christ on a certain day according to their reading of the Bible. They have gone up and down the mountain so many times that they have thrown in the towel and now admit they really don't know when Christ is returning. The point is that a personal "plain" reading of the Bible produces idiosyncrasy and dysfunction, and, too often, tragedy.

So, what is the fundamentalist Bible reader to do? Where can he or she turn for an authoritative interpretation of a puzzling passage? Fundamentalists answer, "To the pastor." Richard De Haan of the Radio Bible Class explains the close connection between the pastor and the biblical text: "Yes, he is a fallible human being, but God has entrusted him with God's infallible word. He therefore has a great message to proclaim and you are under obligation to heed the exhortations and obey the directives which come from the Scriptures through the pastor to you" (Your Pastor and You, p. 18; quoted in Kathleen Boone's *The Bible Tells Them So: The Disclosure of Protestant Fundamentalism*). Or, as Jerry Falwell likes to put it, the pastor is "God's man," and therefore his directives are to be obeyed by the Christian disciple. Well, now, what's this? What do we have here? We have not the pope of Rome. We have as many popes as there are evangelical pastors! Catholics who go over to fundamentalism discover that they have simply exchanged one pope for another—with the exception, if they don't like their local pope's interpretation, they can seek another. Many evangelical ministers wield a power that would make the pope or the local Catholic pastor envious. In extreme cases you get a Jim Jones or David Koresh. The minister, the interpreter of the Bible, wields great power in fundamentalism.

So now we have come full circle. The fundamentalists begin with the claim that the Bible is inspired by God and cannot contain error. It is a plain book that can be understood by plain people who read it with faith; the believer is guided by the Holy Spirit, so there is no need for church authority. Yet the believers are not allowed to interpret the text any way they choose. If they do not have access to the approved commentaries, they are to submit their questions and even their views to the authority of the pastor. "No need for church authority" translates as, "well, of course, you must submit to the minister's authority." In his study of a fundamentalist Christian school, Alan Peshkin quotes a student disgruntled with the quality of church music: "The Bible distinctly says, you know, take trumpets and cymbals and stuff and praise the Lord with that. Over here in [my fundamentalist church], if you don't have just a piano or organ, it's wrong, it's a sin." It is ironic that some Catholics who left the church because they found it too authoritarian are willing to accept an even more rigid authority structure in a fundamentalist church. Even the demand of total allegiance is oppressive. It is not without reason that many returning to the Catholic faith complain that as fundamentalists they had no time for themselves: socials, Wednesday evening services, two on Sunday, Bible studies, youth group, etc., were all-encompassing schedules that demanded conformity or ostracization.

The Catholic View

Anyway, in this whole issue, Catholics heartily agree that the Bible is the inspired Word of God, but, they insist, it is a word that has come down to us through human writers who, as the Second Vatican Council said, "made use of their powers and abilities," and the council encouraged scholars to study the historical, cultural circumstances in which the various books were composed as well as their literary forms. Yes, the Catholic church holds to biblical inerrancy, but unlike the fundamentalists who insist that the Bible is absolutely free of error, the church says that errancy extends only to the religious truths of the Bible. There may well be scientific or historical errors in the Bible and literary exaggerations, but basically who cares? These do not diminish the Bible as the bearer of religious truth. For the fact is that the sacred writers were not interested in teaching science, history, or psychology. Catholics, with the help of tradition, simply separate the kernel of religious truth from the packaging which may or may not be true.

We know, for example, that Jesus made up things that aren't factual. We call them parables. There is no priest, there is no Levite, there are no robbers, there is no Good Samaritan. Jesus made the whole thing up—but within this fable, this story, this parable, is a wonderful truth. Likewise, Catholics have no trouble, say, with accounts of a six-day creation and evolution, for the creation story is not a literal account but the bearer of the great message that God is the Lord and creator of all things, no matter which way it happened. Or that the book of Jonah is not literally true but basically a parable like our Good Samaritan story, both of which say that God will forgive even pagans who repent. The major point Catholics make is such an obvious one: the 5000-year-old Bible, from an entirely different culture, language, and worldview is not always a "plain" book, any more than Shakespeare's 300-year-old plays are "plain." True enough, the ordinary reader can always find inspiration and guidance from reading the Bible prayerfully, just as he or she can gain insight into human nature by reading Shakespeare. But because the Bible, like Shakespeare, can too easily be misunderstood, it needs (at least sometimes) to be clarified and interpreted. Actually, this need for help in interpretation is expressed in the Bible itself. Remember when the Ethiopian official was reading the words of the prophet Isaiah, Philip the deacon asked him, "Do you understand what you are reading?" The man replied, "How can I, unless someone guides me?" (Acts 8:30–31).

Similarly, Catholics have always felt the need for some

guidance in reading the Scriptures because of the all-too-human tendency to misinterpret and misunderstand. One of the letters of Peter also warns about this tendency. Speaking of Paul's letters he says, "There are some things in them hard to understand, which the ignorant and unstable twist to their own destruction, as they do the other Scriptures" (2 Peter 3:16). So, it comes down to this: Catholics, too, rely on the Holy Spirit in reading Scripture, but do so in the context of the ongoing church: the Spirit + that context = Tradition. After all, it is commonplace knowledge, as we have seen, that the church preceded the Scriptures. As someone once put it, "It is the church that gave us the Bible, not the other way around."

Are You Saved?

When all the Bible waving is over, you will be hit with the "Jackpot" question: "Are you saved?" Like the woman who was late for a fundamentalist convention. She slipped into the crowded room and finally spied an empty chair. As she slipped into it, she whispered to the man next to her, "Is this chair saved?" He replied, "No, but we're praying for it." That ubiquitous question revolves around this truth in minds of fundamentalists: all agree that God has forgiven our sins and reconciled us and gives us a firm hope of eternal life and that all this has been won for us through the death and resurrection of Jesus.

The divisive question is, what is our role in all this? How do we "take hold" of the salvation Christ won for us? Fundamentalists answer, "When we make a personal decision to accept Jesus Christ as our Lord and Savior." The typical formula is, "Confess your sins and receive Jesus into your heart." In other words, in a moment of truth and grace, I come to the realization that I am on a downward path spiritually. Feeling the guilt and weight of my own sins (I can't blame anyone else for my own failures), and feeling my utter powerlessness to turn my life around by my own efforts, I come to believe that Jesus Christ gave his life for me on the cross and thereby took away my sins once and for all. I don't have to keep trying so hard to be perfect; all I have to do is commit my life to Christ and let him be my Savior. This is what it means to be "born again."

A number of consequences flow from this theology of salvation. Note, first of all, that the "saving act" is purely an internal one. There is no need for any external ritual or public ceremony. Some fundamentalists do not even believe in the necessity of baptism except as an external sign of the great event that has taken place internally. And nearly all fundamentalists reject infant baptism; they see it as a meaningless ritual, since the baby is incapable of making a conscious commitment to Christ.

Second, fundamentalists believe that once they have made this decisive commitment, their salvation is absolutely assured. This is why they exude such spiritual self-confidence and why they can't understand it when Catholics seem to "waffle" about their assurance of salvation: "Well, gee, I hope I'll be saved, but I suppose I can blow it if I'm not careful." Fundamentalists can't understand such talk. For them, once you accept Jesus Christ into your heart, he will never abandon you. Not even if you go back to a life of sin? No!—your sins cannot invalidate your salvation. The only way you can be lost is to explicitly repudiate your act of commitment to Christ. "Once saved, always saved" is the slogan—even if you live like a pagan and disregard every commandment of God and human decency there is, although in this case they believe that God will send you set-backs, failures, and suffering to call you back to your senses. Still, even then, you will not be lost. (You can't help but sense the undiluted Christian individualism in all of this.)

Catholics do agree that salvation is not a human achievement but also add that it is not a once-and-for-all event but an ongoing process—that would seem common sense—and not only an interior event but includes the public, external rite of baptism. Indeed, you have to have an internal "born again" experience, but, there's what Jesus said, "no one can enter the kingdom of God without being born again of water and the Spirit," and it is overwhelmingly obvious that the early church took these words as referring to baptism. It's all over Scripture: "Go therefore and make disciples of all nations, baptizing them in the name of the Father and of the Son and of the Holy Spirit," and Paul's letters and Acts are filled with accounts of baptisms.

We need both, of course: the external rite and the internal conversion. Catholics must make a conscious commitment to Jesus sometime in their adult life and some do—at retreats, Marriage Encounter, a Cursillo, or a parish mission—and we must do this many times. Salvation is ongoing and we must do good works. Fundamentalists dismiss good works as a sign that you're trying to be saved by your own efforts, but Catholics don't claim that. Catholics simply and scripturally claim that there is an innate connection between belonging to Jesus and acting in accordance with his teaching, a connection clearly stated in the gospels: "If you love me, you will keep my commandments" (John 14:15).

Also, the fundamentalist view of "accepting Jesus as one's personal savior" boldly contradicts Matthew 25, where Jesus gives quite a different criterion for being saved. For there he explicitly says, "Come, you that are blessed by my Father, inherit the kingdom prepared for you from the foundation of the world; for I was hungry and you gave me food; I was thirsty and you gave me something to drink..." And when these righteous ask when did they do these things, Jesus replies, "Just as long as you did it to one of the least of these who are members of my family, you did it to me." On the other hand he condemns as unsaved those who did not do these corporal works of mercy: "And these," he says, "will go away into eternal punishment, but the righteous into eternal life."

Obviously more than an internal commitment to Jesus is needed for salvation. The spiritual and corporal works of mercy must figure in. Also, how about Jesus' words that mercy would be shown to those who show mercy, and, "Not everyone who says Lord, Lord will enter the Kingdom of heaven, but only the one who does the will of my Father in heaven" (Matthew 7:21) and James' famous "faith without works is dead," plus those other words of James, "What good is it, my brothers and sisters, if you say you have faith but do not have works. Can faith save you?" (2:14).

Catholics do have a firm hope of salvation, but not absolute assurance. After all, Jesus cautions, "the love of many will grow cold. But the one who endures will be saved" (Matthew 24:12–13), and Paul says, "Work out your salvation with fear and trembling" (Philippians 2:12), which he wouldn't say if salvation were absolutely assured. And Paul himself says he does penance so that "after proclaiming to others, I myself should become disqualified" (1 Corinthians 9:26–27). As someone has pointed out, fundamentalists seem to confuse salvation with justification. That is, we are justified (made right) with God when we acknowledge Jesus Christ as our Lord and Savior and receive him into our hearts. In this Catholics fully concur in the sense that being "made right" or justified is a total free gift of God with no input from ourselves and is not the result of any "good works" that we do. You can't earn a gift. That is why, in a landmark agreement between Lutherans and Catholics issued in June of 1998, both sides agreed to this formula: divine forgiveness and salvation come only through God's grace. Their joint statement reads:

> All persons depend completely on the saving power of God for their salvation. The freedom they possess in relation to persons and the

things of this world is no freedom in relation to
salvation, for as sinners they stay under God's
judgment and are incapable of turning by themselves to God to seek deliverance, of meriting
their justification before God, or of attaining salvation by their own abilities. Justification takes
place solely by God's grace.

So justification comes solely from God and not by anything
we do. However, "good works flow from that," and, as we
have seen above, there is a definite scriptural connection
between salvation and the corporal works of mercy of
Matthew 25. In short, justified by pure gift is one reality and
"being saved" as a freely justified sinner is another. In other
words, being made righteous by God's pure gift in Christ is
one thing; what that freely, unearned, justified, person does
with his or her life is another. Salvation is an ongoing, lifetime process of conversion, struggle, backsliding, recommit-
ment, seeking forgiveness, and overcoming our demons.
And always, always we know that we are not alone: "I am
with you always," Jesus said, "to the end of the age"
(Matthew 28:20).

The Catholic Mass

The matter of the Catholic Mass has been a great source of
controversy between fundamentalists and Catholics.
Fundamentalists say that the Mass is contrary to the
Scriptures, that Jesus offered only one perfect sacrifice for
our sins and to keep offering more sacrifices is equivalent to
idolatry. They love to quote the passage in Hebrews that
says:

> For Christ did not enter a sanctuary made by
> human hands, a mere copy of the true one, but
> he entered into heaven itself, now to appear in
> the presence of God on our behalf. Nor was it

to offer himself again and again, as the high priest enters the Holy Place year after year with blood that is not his own; for then he would have had to suffer again and again since the foundation of the world. But as it is, he has appeared once for all at the end of the age to remove sin by the sacrifice of himself.

—Hebrews 9:2–26

At first glance this looks like a strong argument against the Catholic Mass. Nevertheless, the context makes it clear that the author is merely contrasting Christ's sacrifice with the Old Testament sacrifices, which had no power to take away sins. He certainly is not talking about the eucharist. Moreover, it is clear from both Scripture (see 1 Corinthians 11:17 ff) and history that Christians in fact gathered to celebrate the eucharist at least weekly, and that they believed they were doing so in obedience to the command of Jesus to "do this in remembrance of me" (Luke 22:19). Furthermore, they believed they were mysteriously (sacramentally) reenacting the one perfect sacrifice of Jesus and were partaking of his true body and blood. How else could Paul make such strong claims?

"For as often as you eat this bread and drink the cup, you proclaim the Lord's death until he comes. Whoever, therefore, eats the bread or drinks the cup of the Lord in an unworthy manner will be answerable for the body and blood of the Lord" (1 Corinthians 11:26–27). As a matter of history, the Catholic church has never taught that in the Mass Jesus is "re-sacrificed" or offered up to suffer again and again. Rather, the Mass is called a sacrifice because in it the unique sacrifice of Christ on Calvary is made real and present to us by God here and now through the visible signs of bread and wine, so that we can enter into this central mystery of our faith in a new way.

Catholic Responses

What are Catholics to do in the face of militant fundamentalism? For one thing, they can learn from it and even admire some of its stances. Fundamentalists have that personal relationship with Christ and are truly "committed to the Lord." Catholics, we must admit, are raised to learn a set of doctrines and follow a set of rules, but not taught to know Jesus. How many Catholics do you hear speak fervently about Jesus as they do the church? We get so preoccupied with revising the liturgy, signing petitions, our own agenda, criticizing the hierarchy, dunning the pastor, leading the opposition, and issues of social justice that we lose the center of it all. What is an outsider's perception of the Catholic church, of Catholics? A power-hungry, male-dominated, misogynist, homophobic, racist church. I think that about covers it! Catholics, we have noted before (and will again) are like everyone else, indistinguishable in every category, reports the Gallup poll, from every other American. But the evangelical fundamentalists? You can spot them a mile away. Listen to actor Robert Duvall who was up for an Academy Award for his remarkable movie *The Apostle*, which he wrote, directed, and starred in. The idea for this movie had been rummaging around in his mind for a while, but what motivated him to bring it to light was an experience. He went down South to flesh out his idea and he thought he'd go into a local church to catch something of the flavor of what was going on. He writes:

> I had never seen such an extraordinary outward expression of faith as I witnessed in the Pentecostal church. I had never seen a church like that. People could barely contain the joy of their faith. Folks were alive with it, imbued. Folks were on their knees singing praises and clapping, shouting to God! The air cracked with

the Spirit. It was impossible to be a mere observer.

When was the last time you felt like that in a Catholic church? He goes on:

I wanted to sing and shout with them. I couldn't explain it, but I knew that people in that church had a gift, a story to share. Somehow, someday, I would tell that story.

He continues,

What was most important to me was to make a movie where Christianity was treated on its own terms, with the respect it deserves. Hollywood usually shows preachers as hucksters and hypocrites, and I was sick and tired of that. I wanted to show the joy and vitality I had seen with my own eyes and felt in my heart and in my life, the sheer, extraordinary excitement of faith. I especially wanted to capture the rich flavor, the infectious cadences and rhythm of good, down home, no-holds-barred preaching. The story seemed to flow from me. I wasn't getting anywhere with Hollywood, yet my work on the movie filled my soul. One Sunday in New York I visited six churches, ending up at Harlem's vast Abyssinian Baptist church. There in a packed congregation before a huge choir, when we all began to sing "What a Friend We Have in Jesus," I found myself connected to the Lord in a way I had never felt before, deep within me. Yes, I thought, we're all kin through Jesus. Not just what we read about him in the Bible, but who he is. That was the secret to powerful faith, the power I wanted to convey in my movie.

It's hard to imagine a Catholic writing those words. Then, too, as we have noted before, the loss of a rich Catholic devotional life has deprived the human spirit of expression, solace, and comfort, for the realistic fact is that the Mass is not enough. It indeed is central, powerful, and defining, but it is no disrespect to say that it is not enough.

We Catholics might emulate the fundamentalist's passion for Scripture. They do put us to shame. People are really hungry for the Word of God, so we should encourage Scripture study in our parishes. But we must have sound leaders and a sound text; otherwise we'll slip into the "Bible alone" mentality of the fundamentalists and certain strong people will, in effect, start a new denomination if separated from the mainstream tradition. There are, as you know, many fine Catholic Bible study courses. Secondly, we must remember that the Bible alone is not sufficient, for after all, we do meet God in other ways. Through nature, through the sacraments, through the church, through ritual and healing, and especially in the eucharist, where we should gather regularly to celebrate "the Lord's Supper," in which we firmly believe we receive the body and blood of the Lord Jesus himself: "The cup of blessing that we bless, is it not a sharing in the blood of Christ? The bread that we break, is it not a sharing in the body of Christ?" (1 Corinthians 10:16).

A welcoming parish is surely a sign of a Christ-centered spirituality. Here the fundamentalists do this well. Show up at one of their churches as a stranger and you will be royally greeted and treated at every step. In contrast, a familiar cry about Catholics is, "The Catholic church is so cold!" No one smiles at you, says welcome, good to see you, or we'd like you to meet our pastor. (Well, not every Catholic wants to wish that on a newcomer.) But our problem is also structural: Catholic parishes are too large and understaffed to project recognition and acceptance.

Then there is evangelization. The constant legal pressure

towards privatization of religion, as the only way to co-exist in a land of diversity has caused most to hide their religion or confine it to church on Sundays. But not fundamentalists. True, their zeal is fueled by the urgency of the endtime to gather as many believers as possible before the rapture. But the zeal is there. "Become a contagious Christian" is their slogan. We'll focus on how to promote Catholic evangelization in a later chapter, but here I simply want to note both the need and the contrast of priorities and approaches between fundamentalists and Catholics.

Finally, we must admit that they are on to something. After all, no person, fundamentalist or not, conservative or liberal, is happy about every aspect of modern society, not the least of which is its incredible ability to permeate, through the pervasive power of advertising and mass media, all of us with one-dimensional secular values. Even good people unthinkingly absorb them (legal abortion or legally assisted suicide, for example, could not exist if the country's sixty million Catholics spoke with one voice). The Catholic church's Pastoral Constitution does say its mission is "to shed on the whole world the radiance of the gospel message, and to unify under one Spirit all people of whatever nature, race, or culture," and it requires that within the church itself there be "mutual esteem, reverence, and harmony" and a "full recognition of lawful diversity." Still, diversity and mutual esteem also require unity and judgment and certain strategies of maintaining Catholic identity and simple human decency. We are rightfully wary of the fundamentalists for their extremes but appreciative of their crying "ouch" when incessantly pricked by the likes of Beavis and Butthead.

Why Do They Turn?

We want to end this chapter with a brief consideration of why people—including Catholics—might turn to fundamentalism (and there are a disproportionate share of Catholics who make up new recruits). We must never dismiss the notion that in fact some are genuine religious seekers. Some have sought answers within the church but have come away dissatisfied. One young man who was struggling with his faith, having been exposed at college to some fundamentalists, writes, "I went to some local Catholic priests to discuss these things, but I found them less helpful than I would have wished (to be frank, I often felt after a little conversation that I was more familiar with the Bible than they)."

Some Catholics have had searing negative experiences that have forced them from the church. More pertinent, however, is that most Catholic converts know very little about their own religion. Over and over again we must state the obvious: religious illiteracy is our biggest problem. We can never underestimate this. In another chapter we'll quote former minister turned Catholic, Scott Hahn, saying how easy it was as a minister to convert Catholics since they were so ignorant of their own beliefs. Later on, as a Catholic teacher in a Catholic college, he was still astounded at the high level of ignorance.

Compounding this, some have had little example at home or come from only-occasionally practicing Catholic homes. Some are disillusioned about their own faith or are searching for community. Others have deeply rooted social and family-related difficulties. We know, for example, that family relationships prior to joining a cult or sect are often pivotal factors. As one psychologist says,

> Children who receive double messages from their parents, who have a poor father-child relationship, who are beset with sexual pressures and the demands of adulthood, and who have strong dependency needs (which are sometimes satisfied by drugs) are said to be among the more likely candidates for membership in a

marginal religious group.

The changing family and social structures are a pressure point. Certainly, a critical point among young adults is when they are going through a major transition (such as going away to college) or other crisis in their lives, like the loss of a parent through death. You can guarantee that some fundamentalist on campus is there at the right time and right place to offer promises of help, peace, and happiness—and just the right solution for their problems. And to bring together people who want to share a common lifestyle: in effect, the offer of community. Uncertain youth are prime targets for confident leaders. In extreme cases, vulnerable children and teens are highly susceptible to cults and Satanism, and, sadly, as we are well aware, of venting their rage by killing classmates and teachers.

Here we might interject an aside for parents for whom a child's joining a sect or cult or an Eastern religion or a fundamentalist one, can be trying. Such parents suffer a loss, and guilt—are they partly to blame for what has happened?—and the fear that a loved one is on the wrong spiritual path, all honest emotions. They may need counseling to help them understand the conscious or unconscious motivations behind their child's decision. But the professional advice is: do continue to love them, especially family members. But also do be firm if they, in extreme cases, are disruptive, upsetting or pressuring other family members. Sometimes, in order to justify their new commitments, they may turn to criticizing their parents or attacking the mainline churches. If they've joined a fundamentalist church, try to affirm the good you see happening in their lives: more prayerful, more-faith-filled, more devoted. But, on the other hand, don't be blind to their sometimes intolerance, self-righteousness, or their imbalance, for example, giving too much time to the church while neglecting their families or becoming joyless and grim.

We should avoid arguments and "Bible shoot-outs" with fundamentalists. You'll never win; they'll always come back with another quote. Just ask them some questions and give them some Scripture quotes to think about. They may fire back with what they have learned, but the questions will stick. Especially, above all, avoid discussions with ex-Catholics who are now fundamentalists. It's as no-win situation. As Scott Hahn points out, "Unlike typical anti-Catholic Protestants, who enjoy nothing more than intense biblical debates over Catholic issues like Mary and the pope, the ex-Catholic fundamentalists we would run into were filled with such rage and resentment toward the church that it rendered them incapable of rational discourse."

So, what's the best approach? Simply affirm your own faith—learn about it. After all, they—the opposition—read all the time material ranging from the Bible to favorite standard anti-Catholic books like Lorraine Boettner's four hundred-page *Roman Catholicism*, which demonstrates that the Catholic church is unbiblical and full of "heresies and inventions," including prayers for the dead, the sign of the cross, veneration of the angels, daily Mass, holy water, the exaltation of Mary, Purgatory, the papacy, and lots more. And very few Catholics can respond and not a few are convinced by the book. Such books and endless pamphlets exposing the "evils" of Catholicism can be very persuasive for Catholics who do not know their own tradition and who aren't sure why they believe what they believe.

Our parting words in this chapter and a bridge to the next are that ironically, fundamentalism has, as we hinted at the beginning, one affinity with its enemy, the New Age. They are both intricately tied into the apocalyptic mentality and script. More than ever, both are revving up their rhetoric and spewing forth tons of books and pamphlets. The cause of all this? The year 2000 is at hand. And, perhaps as you read this, that year has come and gone. It makes no difference. The fascination with the end of the world, as we shall see, remains, regardless of dates and times. To this fascination we must now turn.

5

The End Is Near—Always!

The end crowns all;
And that old common arbitrator, Time,
Will one day end it.
—Shakespeare

A well-known speaker often gave a lecture entitled, "On the Nature of the Universe." One night after he had delivered it in a small town, an elderly woman confronted him, saying, "That was a brilliant lecture, but you have it all wrong. The universe is not as you described it. Earth, for example, is not a little ball moving around the sun. Our world is just a crust of earth on the back of a huge turtle." Very gently the speaker replied, "That is an interesting theory, but tell me: what is the turtle standing on?" The woman replied, "I see that you are a very intelligent man, and that is an intelligent question, but I've got the answer. The turtle is standing on the back of a much larger turtle." The speaker patiently asked, "And what is the second turtle standing on?" To which the woman replied, "It's no use, it's turtles all the way down!"

Welcome to the world of the Apocalypse, where turtle theories abound. For those of you unfamiliar with this arcane world, you are about to encounter concepts, language, and notions that range from the sensible to the silly, the wary to the wild, the abstract to the absurd, the calculating to the opportunistic. Did you know that M&Ms have been declared the official candy of the millennium? Or that New York City has been declared by the *New York Times* as "Millennium Central," the place to be on the first day of the century?

So let me begin this chapter lightly by giving fair warning that I am about to pull a dirty trick, equivalent to giving you a fabulous mystery novel—and then, before you read it, telling you who the murderer is. Since the topic is "The End Is Near!," the usual tack is to lay out the clues for this great happening which is imminent (it is always imminent) and even, in line with a very long tradition, to pinpoint the date. But my dirty trick is this: to announce to you the fact that the end of the world has already come and gone. So to speak.

Facts about the Millennium

You see, as everyone knows, the western calendar that we follow has undergone so many revisions that when the numbers dust finally settled, we found that we're off three to seven years in our calculations. Jesus Christ, whose birth the millennium is all about (we forget too easily that the year 2000 is the 2000th anniversary of that birth), was really born around 4 B.C. That would place the 2000th year of his birth in 1997, which means, at this writing (1999) the millennium has come and gone and so has the predicted end of the world. Not to mention that in the Muslim world, this is the year 1419. And, if you want to get technical, consider this: since a millennium is a period of a thousand years, the year 1 was the first year of the first millennium, and the year 1001 was the first year of the second millennium, and therefore the year 2000 will be the last year of the second millennium not the first year of the third millennium. All those who use it as the marker for apocalyptic doings are off a year.

Anyway, as Stephen Jay Gould points out, the very term millennium has pretty much changed from a religious concept concerning the Second Coming of Jesus to a mere mat-ter-of-fact designation for the end of a 1000-year period. The very simple, logical reason for this is that all predictions about the Second Coming—and there are endless numbers of them—have failed, as we shall see. As J. Gordon Melton, head of the Institute for the Study of American Religion, has commented, "Everyone who predicted the end of the world had one thing in common. They were wrong." (As I write these words I am staring at a large headline from the *Biblical Prophecy Corner* entitled: "Why I Expect the Rapture on Pentecost, 1998." Note that you are reading this after May 31, 1998, thus verifying Melton's observation. I call it "Melton's Law.")

But this fact does not deter the devotees of the endtime, for any year that ends with three zeros, whether correct or not, is too rare, too exotic, not to make something of it. As a panel of Bible-reading, Dead Sea Scroll experts proclaimed in May of 1995, in the supermarket tabloid, *The Weekly World News*, the world will definitely end on December 31st, 1999.

However, we should note the novelty of even noticing the millennium at all. The very notion of using seconds, min-utes, and centuries as a means of universal orientation arrived very late on the scene. Outside of monasteries in the medieval period, time was not marked by calendars. Most people were totally unaware of the existence of the Anno Domini calendar. Until the eighteenth century only official documents noted A.D. (a designation recently deleted from all official government and civic documents at the behest of a couple of lawyers who claimed that it violated the separa-tion of church and state).

It was only in the thirteenth century that there was any notion at all of marking the end of a century. This was Pope Boniface VIII's Jubilee Year, a celebration which he orga-nized (although he declared it was a tradition), thus pioneering a custom which we observe to this day, as is the case with the Year of Jubilee proclaimed by Pope John Paul II. Protestant reaction to Roman "deviations" led their scholars to publish the *Magdeburg Centuries* in sixteen volumes (never completed), one for each century. These set the precedent for conceiving time in terms of centuries, one following another. Thus only from the sixteenth century on do we really have measured time. Our assumptions about a new or old millennium are really our own conceits.

Some Not Impressed

Be that as it may, let it be noted that, no matter what, some cynics are not impressed with all the zeros nor with the fact that a new millennium has arrived (or come and gone). James Finn Garner in his book, *Apocalypse Wow*, for example, notes that the millennium really makes little difference. He writes that in the year 999, there was an ignorant, illiterate population relying on privileged, self-serving demagogues to interpret the world around them; a millennium later, we have "24-hour talk radio." In 999, the Vikings would invade settlements, plunder populations, and destroy local European culture; a millennium later, the world is overrun by satellite TV and McDonald's. In 999, there were tubercular peasants dressed in rags and covered with mud, filth, and grime; a millennium later, we have models in *Details* magazine. In 999, people lived in rickety huts and lean-tos, constantly fearful of attack; a millennium later, people live in 10-room houses in gated communities, constantly fearful of attack.

Other writers point out that yes, the year 2000 will bring chaos (has brought, if you're reading this after that date) but not in terms of any religious global conflagration preceding the thousand-year reign of Christ. Instead, the chaos will be in the very mundane terms of a severe blow to the economy, because all of the computers will be out of whack (what's called the Y2K problem). In the early days of computer-making, memory space was so costly that programmers used only two digits to indicate a year. So, for example, 75 represented 1975, and 86 represented 1986. Now the problem is that in the year 2000 these computer systems will continue to register only the last two digits, namely 00, representing 1900! And, later on, 1901, 1902, and so on, causing a major crisis as the computer chips "think" in terms of a hundred years ago and spout out data for those past years.

On the practical level, this means that the parking garage you drove into a few hours ago may think you've been parked since 1900 and charge you accordingly. The elevators may not work. Air traffic computers and communication systems will be in a tizzy. One state prison computer, set to release some prisoners in the year 2000, now tells the warden that the prisoners should have been released in 1900. Some credit card companies have already recalled cards with the expiration date of 2000, thinking that they expired during the McKinley administration.

The Religious Timetable

More seriously, notwithstanding the frenzied scriptural arithmetic of some American evangelicals, the impulse to read "the signs of the [end]times," regardless of what year or century or millennium we're in, goes back long before the present age, long before Christianity, even long before Judaism. The ancient Persian Zoroastrian religion, for example, envisaged an end to history after a final cosmic struggle of good and evil. Such searchings are rooted in the conviction that there is a God, and, consequently, that there is a divine plan. In that plan somewhere there is a divine timetable for the human race, and it is not unreasonable for human beings to try to discern it.

Usually that divine plan is envisaged as falling into certain time frames, or epochs, or kingdoms, or a Great Week:

whatever measurement is used. Certain catastrophes such as floods or earthquakes or wars mark them off—all leading to a cleansing (the destruction of the evil and the saving or rapture of the saved) in preparation for a return to a Golden Age or a New Age of love and fulfillment. For the Hebrews the scenario was cast in a succession of covenant renewals after divine punishments for disobedience. If we but knew such a plan or timetable, we could align ourselves with it and thereby conform to God's will.

That, in a nutshell, is a rationale for believers. For unbelievers, however, for whom there is no God, no plan, human or divine, no purpose to human existence but only accident and randomness and ultimately nothingness, all this discernment is hilarious "sound and fury." Indeed, they have reason to snicker at the solemn silliness not to mention the bizarre behavior of history's "prophets," some of whom were quite pathological. And yet, the religious impulse behind it all is basically sound.

Well, whatever our view, and beyond the severe economic inconveniences we just mentioned, the fact is that a millennium will be a source of anxiety or joy to many—although there is really no widespread "millennium fever," as some like to describe it. Any millennium concerns that arise are flourishing mainly among the fundamentalist religions which are busy scaring the wits out of people. Their fevered preachers, perennially dipping into the Bible's most exotic and difficult books—the book of Daniel and the book of Revelation—proclaim that they have read rightly the mysterious signs therein. They claim that they can predict the day and the hour when Christ will return again, signaling a terrible devastation for the world. No one but no one will be saved—except, of course, those who believe as they do. These believers will be snatched or "raptured" into heaven in the nick of time, while the rest of humanity is destroyed.

Looking for a Reason

When things go wrong, people look to divine aid or at least for divine meaning in it all. Are these tragedies (the Crusades, the Great Schism, the Black Death, etc.) a sign of one epoch ending and another beginning? When you hear such questions in a time of crisis, you are into apocalypticism: reading the signs of the endtime. And, to be truthful, apocalypticism was often the only psychological framework available to deal with massive tragedy. How else to explain things? When terrible things happened, like the devastating sack of Rome in 410 (which for us would be like the invasion of Washington, D.C. by a foreign army), endtimers not only knew it was the end of the world; they knew why it was ending: it fit in with the divine plan.

Apocalypticism, therefore, is a category born out of crisis time. Conflict is the engine that drives it, a conflict based on the old and enduring Persian dualism, showcasing the age-old battle between good and evil, light and darkness, between Arthur and Mordred, Holmes and Moriarity, Luke Skywalker in his white suit and Darth Vader in his black suit, Simba and Uncle Scar, Christ and Antichrist. The inevitable dance of terror and bliss is its scenario: destruction and reward, trial and attainment, endurance and compensation ("But the one who endures to the end will be saved" Matthew 24:13), conflagration and rapture, death and resurrection. It's underground literature, if you will, the literature of those under threat, of those psychologically disoriented by rapid change or disintegration. It's the consolation of the politically, socially, or religiously persecuted (and not just physically but also morally: how do you live with "secular humanism," legal abortion, a drug culture, and pornography on the Internet?). It's Eliza Doolittle's, "Just you wait, 'enry Higgins, just you wait!" Someday things will be reversed and we'll be rewarded and you'll be punished.

Mary sang a similar theme in her Magnificat: "You have

scattered the proud in the thoughts of their hearts. You have brought down the powerful from their thrones and lifted up the lowly" (Luke 1:51–52). Her Son inveighed: "But woe to you who are rich, for you have received your consolation. Woe to you who are full now, for you will be hungry. Woe to you who are laughing now, for you will mourn and weep" (Luke 6:24–25). And, just maybe, we even know when this will happen and you don't, because we've got the code, the key to the books which unlock the secrets of the endtime. It may be the book of Daniel or the book of Revelation or the Fatima secrets. Apocalypticism, then, is the religion of the outsider. It is resistance literature.

Signs of Belief

Still, we must not underestimate the vast numbers of people who are concerned about the end of the world. A *U.S. News & World Report* survey found that most Americans believe the world will end and end soon. Many are into "prophecy" and the endtime business, people ranging from the Divine Metaphysical Research group who met in Washington in 1994, to prepare for the world to end in 1996, to those who have constructed elaborate networks of underground living accommodations in many parts of the country. According to the *Millennial Prophecy Report*, there are eleven hundred groups in the world that believe the end is imminent.

Such beliefs flourish in particular among the evangelicals and fundamentalists, such as the fifteen million Southern Baptists, the Pentecostals, the Jehovah's Witnesses (founded 1884) and its offspring, the Seventh Day Adventists, whose very name means "coming," Assemblies of God (founded 1914), the Mormons, the Worldwide Church of God, and others. Such peoples are to be found largely in the south and in southern California. However, with the spread of cable TV, prophecy and endtime beliefs are not confined to the unlettered or disinherited or lower middle class people, but now find a home in middle class America. It is worth noting, for example, that fifty percent of U.S. college graduates await Jesus Christ's return.

Newsletters, albums (Barry Maguire's 1965 hit, *The Eve of Destruction*; David Bowie's *We've Got Five More Years*; and Aphrodite's Child, *666*, to name a few), websites, magazines, bumper stickers ("Beam me up, Lord"), and books on prophecy and endtime interpretations and scenarios are beyond counting. To mention the more spectacular there is Hal Lindsey's 1970 bestseller, *The Late Great Planet Earth*, which by 1990 had sold 28 million copies (and was also made into a movie featuring commentator Orson Welles); Salem Kirban's *Guide to Survival* (half a million copies); Paul Billheimer's 1975 *Destined for the Throne;* John Walvoord's 1974 *Armageddon, Oil and the Middle East Crisis* (750,000 copies); David Willkerson's 1985 *Set the Trumpet to Thy Mouth* (more than a million copies); and Edgar Whisentant's 2 million-copy bestseller, *88 Reasons Why the Rapture Will Be in 1988*. (Melton's Law once more verified!)

Outside of Lindsey, most of these names are probably unknown to you, but they provide a staple diet for millions of prophecy and endtime devotees. (Practical proof of popularity? The big publishing houses who could care less about prophecy, but care a lot about profits, are eyeing the market: ABC bought Word Books, an evangelical house, and Harper and Row bought Zondervan, a major prophecy publisher.) This is not to mention the chief purveyor of millennium teaching, the famous *Schofield Reference Bible* (1909) which, as we mentioned in the last chapter, is the standard reference for fundamentalist ministers today and has probably sold over twelve million copies. To further underscore the popularity and volume of apocalyptic themes, note that an international team of scholars has gathered to prepare a 1,500 page, three-volume work called *The Encyclopedia of Apocalypticism*, in time for the year 2000.

The New Jerusalem

But America is no stranger to apocalypticism. Prophecy and millennialism came to our own country at its very conception. For the Pilgrim Fathers, the founding of the American colonies was in itself a sign of the endtime. America was soon being identified as the New Jerusalem and even, some contended, the actual place for the appearance of Christ at the endtime. Increase and Cotton Mather were influential preachers of eschatalogical themes, constantly setting dates for the coming of Christ: 1697, 1716, and 1736. The "Great Awakening" of the early eighteenth century was clearly a sign to many Protestant ministers, like the influential Jonathan Edwards, that the Kingdom of God was at hand.

This idea was further abetted in their minds by the French-Indian and Revolutionary Wars, for they read into the latter all kinds of literal fulfillments of Scripture. Burgoyne's invasion from Canada, for example, was seen as a fulfillment of the prophet Joel's prophecy of invaders from the north; Cornwallis' surrender as a link to the millennium. According to the Methodist preacher colorfully named Fountain Pitts, even the Declaration of Independence was foretold in the book of Daniel. And, following the course laid down by Savonarola (whom we'll discuss later), the prosperity and international influence of the New Land was a sign that America might indeed be the New Israel. In short, the millennium, the apocalyptic strain is endemic to America.

But, to move to the present time, the dream of an American Promised Land soured for some who felt that this vision of America was being undermined by Catholics, Jews, or blacks. This suspicion gave way to the activities of the Klu Klux Klan and other hate groups. There were always, of course, small separatist communes springing up which tried to create the perfect conditions for the perfect life, a kind of spiritual communism. These were, in effect, millennial communities, meant to be paradigms of a "perfect society," smaller reflections of the larger separatist Mormons, Jehovah's Witnesses, and Seventh Day Adventists. Some, like the ill-fated Millerites, specifically formed a community around the apocalyptic themes of the endtime.

In more recent times, however, especially in the 1970s and 80s, some of these fringe groups sprang from the soil of the "survivalist" mentality. This mentality was based on a deep distrust of civil authority and an even deeper suspicion of an evil government which (it was an "article of faith") was part of a global conspiracy to take away individual rights. (The conspiracy motif permeates all fringe groups. Remember in Catholic circles Archbishop Lefebvre's movement which saw "the liberal plot of Satan against Church and Papacy alike." In fact, it was contended that Pope Paul VI, who presided at the end of the council, was not the real pope at all. He was a fake, an imposter, and so all the resolutions of Vatican Council II are null and void. The throne of St. Peter remains open until the advent of a traditionalist pope.)

Only "true believers" can contend with such evil forces. This mentality has, in turn, spawned small enclaves all over the country, often heavily armed, to resist the encroachments of the government, the enemy of freedom, which is seen as part of a vast international conspiracy. The bombing at Oklahoma City fits perfectly into this mentality. Other like-minded armed communities often turned to endtime scenarios, like the Bible-quoting, self-declared messiah, David Koresh, and his ill-fated Davidian community at Waco, Texas.

Ancient Roots

In both the old and and new worlds prophecy and apocalyptic thinking have survived underground because they have such a long history. (As we explore this history, we fall into murky waters, but bear with me.) Long before

Christianity, foretelling the future was a huge cottage industry. The ancient Greeks had the sibyl. Sibyl is the name of a legendary pagan prophetess; more accurately, sybil is more a title or an office, like the word guru, applying to anyone who fills the job. The most famous Sibylline Oracle was at Delphi. The sibyl (usually a woman), like the fortune tellers of today, would "predict" events that had already happened or couch her replies in such ambiguous terms that she would be right no matter how things turned out. These oracles were continually being added to throughout the centuries, so that we now have *The Sibylline Oracles*, a collection of fifteen books in Greek verse containing pagan, Jewish, and, finally, Christian material from various periods of history.

You can tell the influence at work in the oracle by looking at its target. For example, terrible predictions against Greek and later Roman occupation indicate an Asian or Jewish hand. Book Three dates back to around 140 B.C., and is a Jewish book describing the coming of the Messiah. Christians used it to find hints of the prediction of Christianity, especially in the volume called *Tiburtina* or *Tibertine Oracle,* an oracle which, as we shall see later, even foretold that the Jews would eventually turn to Christ. That's why the haunting medieval hymn Dies Irae speaks of "Teste David cum Sibylla"—both the Jewish King David and the pagan Sibyl testifying to Jesus. This also explains why Michelangelo painted the Delphic Sibyl on the ceiling of the Sistine chapel.

Apocryphal Writings

Jewish apocrypha (non-canonical or unapproved books) flourished. They detailed forthcoming events and the destruction of this or that kingdom or the world, making them apocalyptic writings as well. In apocryphal writing someone always has a vision or is caught up to heaven and brings back secrets, especially secrets revealing the endtime and who is or is not going to be saved. Examples of such books are 3 Baruch, the disciple of the prophet Jeremiah, (they always appended the name of a biblical celebrity to give the book credence), 1 Enoch (at first accepted by the Christian church as canonical but later rejected), 2 Enoch, the Psalms of Solomon, the Assumption of Moses (this contains the legend of Satan and the archangel Michael arguing over the body of Moses; the Epistle of Jude in the New Testament will repeat this story), 2 Esdras, and 4 Esdras. The books of David were written at the height of the Maccabean revolt (165 B.C.). The Apocalypse of Baruch and Ezra (first century B.C.) replaced the wise Messiah with a superhuman warrior king; the book of Jubilees was found among the Dead Sea scrolls.

Many messiahs appeared in the troubled days before the destruction of the Temple in 70 A.D. Even in the last great Jewish uprising in 131 A.D., its leader, Simon Bar Kokhba, was hailed as the true Messiah. The above books and others were written mostly from the third to the first century B.C., and even at the time of Jesus. Understandably, messianic prophecy intensified as the political lot of the Jews became more intolerable. All such prophecies profess to reveal secrets to those who can read the symbols. They all "foretell" events, and all include some predictions of the end, either of this or that (oppressing) kingdom or the world itself, and the establishment of a new order.

Ezekiel and Isaiah

Of course, the canonical or approved books that found their way into the Old Testament are not free of apocalyptic writings. The prophetic literature, in particular, mentions a millennial kingdom which, after a cosmic holocaust in which Yahweh will triumph over his enemies, will be ruled over by a "Deliverer" and a "saved" remnant of Israel. (As we shall see, this is exactly the scenario of the Christians who replaced Deliverer with Jesus and the remnant with the raptured.) You find statements such as the following: All people will drink of the cup of God's wrath (Jeremiah 25:15–29); Yahweh will deliver the wicked to the sword (Jeremiah 25:30–38); the godless armies will be annihilated (Ezekiel 39:1–7); and all nations will see the glory of God and the divine judgment (Ezekiel 39:21).

These latter references from Ezekiel remind us that, in fact, our oldest example of apocalyptic biblical literature most likely goes back to Ezekiel's time, to the trauma of the Babylonian exile (sixth century B.C.), the fall of the Temple, and the collapse of the monarchy. (For Catholics this would be like the invasion of Rome, the razing of St. Peter's, and the capture of the pope.) Such unspeakable catastrophes cast doubt as to whether salvation was any longer possible within history. Similarly, during the Holocaust some Jews had their faith shaken as a Chosen People.

Although the book of Ezekiel thought salvation was possible within history, it provides fantastic, extravagant imagery that pushes beyond history. In doing so it feeds the apocalyptic imagination with other-worldly solutions, usually nothing short of annihilation and starting all over again with a golden age (in Christian thought, the thousand-year glorious rule of Christ; more of this later). Indeed, most of the language and images for future apocalyptic writing would come from Ezekiel.

It is in Ezekiel's thirty-seventh chapter, for example, that we find the vision of the dry bones coming to life and the prediction of the fate awaiting the heathen "in the latter days." Chapter 8 begins, "Son of Man, set thy face against Gog and Magog, the chief prince of Meschech and Tubal and prophesy against him....Gog.... together with Persia, Ethiopia and Libya...the house of Togarmah of the north quarters, and all his bands," will invade Israel as part of the divinely permitted punishment on Israel for its sins. But finally the Lord will drive away and punish the invaders. He will do this with pestilence, blood, and fire falling on the land of Magog. Then the Lord promises to bring back a chastised Israel to Judea again.

I mention this prophecy in particular because it plays such a big part in fundamentalist prophecy. "Gog and Magog" figure as hated enemies of Israel. They come from the north to invade Israel, bringing destruction and suffering, but they themselves will ultimately be defeated. Prophecy people have a great time identifying Gog and Magog, usually the "enemy" in any period of history; you'll find those names constantly in prophetic literature. The Jews equated Gog with the Scythians; St. Augustine saw Gog as representing all unbelievers. With the rise of the Ottoman empire in the late thirteenth century, the Turks became Gog, and the idea of the Turk as Gog remained in force a long time and is still present in Greek lore today.

In our time there is a new contender who will invade Israel: Gog is identified with Russia (as Meshech is identified with Moscow). Not only does Russia lie to the north of Palestine but, with the Bolshevik revolution of 1917, the repudiation of Christianity, and the public espousal of atheism, the identification seemed to be natural. (Hal Lindsey's blockbuster has a chapter cleverly entitled, "When Russia is A Gog.") This interpretation was a favorite when communism existed. It had to be revised somewhat when the Cold War ended and communism fell.

A similarly cosmic vision is sketched by Isaiah (24–27) and in Daniel (2 and 7). A kingless Jerusalem is identified as the focal point of God's new reign over Israel, and it is to the mountain of God (Zion) in Jerusalem that all nations will stream (Micah 4:1–4; Isaiah 2:2–4).

The Book of Daniel

Again, this kind of vision was gradually transferred from early earthly victory and triumph to a heavenly one. The oft-quoted book of Daniel (the one containing our favorite stories of King Belshazzar's feast, Daniel in the lion's den, Shadrach, Meschach, and Abednego in the fiery furnace, and the story of Susanna and the wicked men) is a good example of this vision. Its message is that God is in charge and will achieve God's will and intervene without any cooperation from human persons. Inevitably, the precise time of such an intervention becomes a preoccupation; in the same book of Daniel we see attempts to pinpoint it. The countdown in Daniel is determined by the division of history into specific periods (later revived in modern evangelical Protestantism as "dispensations" or time periods): the four empires; weeks or years or jubilees; seven times seven; seventy shepherds of the people; and so on.

Few passages in Scripture have spawned as much speculation as Daniel's seventy days or weeks or years, whatever they might mean. There is always a schema to be interpreted. It is worth noting here that the book of Daniel purports to be written in the sixth century B.C. at the time of the Babylonian captivity but was actually written four hundred years later (around 167 B.C.). It was easy, in a predated book, to make "predictions" about the future. By the way, Daniel borrowed his concept of successive kingdoms from the Babylonians. He says these kingdoms are Babylon, the Medes and Persians, and the Greeks—except that he has them in the wrong chronological order. But they are the "evil empire," a phrase borrowed by former President Ronald Reagan, who leaned toward apocalypticism. Daniel even refers to an evil "King of the North." This would someday appeal to those who identified the evil empire with Russia, which is north of the Holy Land.

"Crisis" Literature

Of course, the telltale signs of divine intervention are there for all to see: earthquakes, falling stars, confusion, wars, the fall of rulers and princes, etc. You can see why apocalyptic literature is called crisis literature: whenever something terrible happens on a large scale, people give up on any here-and-now solution as hopeless (usually the here-and-now has caused the problem). They look to cosmic, beyond-the-earth solutions ranging from the Second Coming of Christ to an invasion by UFOs. This also explains why modern apocalyptic folk would seize on World War I or II, the atom bomb, economic confusion, and scud missiles as sure signs "foretold" in Scripture as portending the end of time.

Basically, the whole concept of the endtime came from some Jewish radicals of the first century who believed in a Great Week that would be brought to an end by the arrival of the Messiah in 6,000 years. The 6,000 comes from the six-day week (not counting the Sabbath rest), the first day being the act of creation. Since each day represents a thousand years (a reference to one of the psalms), when the week is over, that is, when creation is finished, so is the world. An early second-century Christian document called the Epistle of Barnabas repeats this scenario, predicting the end of the world in the sixth millennium from the beginning of creation.

The New Testament

The New Testament inherited all this as did its contemporary movement, the community at Qumran where the Dead Sea scrolls were discovered. The New Testament is filled with apocalyptic writing or mention of a Second Coming. Of its twenty-seven books only five contain no reference to the return of Jesus. Not surprisingly. The Christians, like the

Jews of old, were experiencing persecution at the hands of the Romans, and readily turned to Jewish apocalypticism to express their plight. The gospels identified Jesus with the Son of Man foretold in Daniel's vision.

In fact, the very first writing in the New Testament, Paul's first letter to the Thessalonians, is all about the endtime and the imminent coming of Christ. Some people were worried that they were still alive and had not yet witnessed the Second Coming. Paul writes:

> For this we declare to you by the word of the Lord, that we who are alive, who are left until the coming of the Lord, will by no means precede those who have died. For the Lord himself, with a cry of command, with the archangel's call and with the sound of God's trumpet, will descend from heaven, and the dead in Christ will first rise. Then we who are alive, who are left, will be caught up in the clouds [raptured] together with them to meet the Lord in the air; and so we will be with the Lord forever. (1 Thessalonians 4:15–17)

It can't be clearer than that. St. Paul fervently believed that the Second Coming was around the corner.

In John's gospel Jesus says, "Do not let your hearts be troubled. Believe in God. Believe also in me. In my Father's house there are many dwelling places. If it were not so, would I have told you that I go to prepare a place for you? And if I go and prepare a place for you, I will come again and will take you to myself so that where I am, there you may also be" (14:1–3).

In Matthew's gospel the disciples asked Jesus the age-old, frequently asked question, "Tell us, when will this be, and what will be the sign about your coming and of the end of the age?" Jesus answered with warnings of false messiahs, insurrections, persecution, and terrible, catastrophic events. Then Jesus added in standard Old Testament symbolic language, "Immediately after the suffering of those days, the sun will be darkened and the moon will not give its light; the stars will fall from the heavens, and the power of heaven will be shaken and...all will see the Son of Man coming on the clouds of heaven. And he will send out his angels with a loud trumpet call, and they will gather his elect from the four winds, from one end of heaven to the other." Then Jesus speaks those fateful words, "When you see all these things, know that he is near, at the very gates. Truly I tell you, this generation [referring to a period of 20-30 years] will not pass away till all these things have taken place" (Matthew 24:29–35).

In the next verse he does say that no one knows the time except the Father, but the nearness motif sticks as Jesus' warning in Mark 13:37 pithily says, "What I say to you, I say to all: Keep awake." Even in the Lord's Prayer, many scholars say that "lead us not into temptation" should properly read, "and keep us from the Ordeal," that is, from the trials at the end of the world.

The angels in Acts 1:11 tell the gaping apostles, "Men of Galilee, why do you stand looking up toward heaven? This Jesus, who has been taken up from you into heaven, will come in the same way as you saw him go in to heaven." Certainly Jesus' resurrection was seen as part of the apocalyptic context, as St. Paul claimed that Christ was "the first fruits of those who have died" (1 Corinthians 15:20).

The never popular and difficult Letter of Jude is quite apocalyptic (and negative). The author writes fiercely of the ungodly people, drawing on invectives from the Jewish apocryphal book, 1 Enoch, which we mentioned above. Jude's reference, by the way, to an apocryphal book caused some hesitation about including his letter in the New Testament canon. But, after all, he says, they were foretold as indicators of the last times.

The pseudonymous Second Letter of Peter, the last book of the New Testament to be written, speaks of the imminent parousia or coming of Christ. In 3:3–5, the author scoffs at those false teachers who are denying the promise of the parousia even though God's inscrutable time is not our time (3:8–10). In the eyes of the Lord, he says, referring to Psalm 90:4, a thousand years are as one day. And if there is a delay, it's only because the Lord is so forbearing and allows time for repentance. Still, sooner or later, that dreadful final day will come.

Finally we come to the work of prophecy, warning, and exotic imagery: the book of Revelation or the Apocalypse, which stands at the very end of the New Testament—although it was not the last New Testament book to be written (2 Peter, remember, has that distinction). Revelation is the New Testament book used most by fundamentalists who claim to decode the fantastic symbolism of the book as a guide to the end of the world. The book itself and the spirit of the times in which it was written easily identified the Antichrist with the hated Roman state, that "ten-horned Beast." It is also noteworthy, as Scripture scholar Raymond Brown points out, that only one passage in this book—containing two verses—mentions the millennium, but what a movement has developed from such small beginnings!

Roman Catholics proclaim their belief in the Second Coming: in the Creed Catholics recite every Sunday: "He will come again to judge the living and the dead"; in the memorial acclamation of the liturgy: "Christ has died, Christ has risen, Christ will come again"; in the third Eucharistic Prayer: "Father, calling to mind the death your Son endured for our salvation, his glorious resurrection and ascension into heaven, and ready to greet him when he comes again"; and in the fourth Eucharistic Prayer: "We recall Christ's death, his descent among the dead, his resurrection and his ascension to your right hand; and, looking forward to his coming in glory…"

A Matter of Record

It's a matter of record—as is "Melton's Law"—that throughout recorded history people have "looked forward" to the Lord's coming persistently and fulsomely. I checked out one source on the Internet and got fifteen pages of close print listing the dates that were supposed to have marked the end of the world! And let me note here the enormous power of the Internet whose news groups relating to prophecy are among the busiest. It serves as a continuous springboard for endtime rumors, especially as the year 2000 approaches (or has come and gone by the time you read this). Here are some samples to give you a taste and introduce you to some key names.

From Justin Martyr to Hildegard of Bingen

156. We should note, first of all, that some early church fathers taught millenarianism, and some were advocates of the endtime scenario, among them eminent theologians such as Justin Martyr, Irenaeus, Lactantius, and Tertullian. To cite one example, a former pagan priest named Montanus began to proclaim a new outpouring of the Holy Spirit and the descent of the heavenly Jerusalem on the Phrygian village of Pepuza. Two of his female prophets, Priscilla and Maximila, even told people the world would end in their lifetime. When they both died and nothing happened, Tertullian rescued the notion of the Second Coming by saying that just as Jesus could not come the first time until all the Old Testament prophecies had been fulfilled, so he cannot come a second time till all prophecies would be fulfilled. Montanus' views spread widely but his teaching was finally condemned by Pope Zephyrinus.

500. In the third century a Roman priest predicted that Christ would return in the year 500, a figure based on the dimensions of Noah's ark.

1132. The so-called "Prophecies of St. Malachy" appears, a list of 112 popes identified by mottoes, which stretches from 1143 until the second Peter, the pope of the endtime. Attributed to Malachy, the twelfth-century Archbishop of Armagh, it is actually a sixteenth-century forgery.

1169. Hildegard of Bingen, the brilliant German abbess, recorded her visions of endtime events in her work, *Scivias*, which is filled with apocalyptic images of towers and fires. A sample: she sees in her first vision "a great mountain the color of iron and enthroned on it One of such great glory that it blinded my sight. On each side of him there extended a soft shadow. Before him, at the foot of the mountain stood an image full of eyes on all sides, in which, because of those eyes, I could discern no human form." The "full of eyes" imagery is straight out of Ezekiel. She also writes of standard familiar themes:

> The Catholic faith wavers among the nations, the mighty books go unread from shameful apathy; and the food of life, the Scriptures, cools to tepidity.... After this, I looked and, behold, all the elements and creatures were shaken by dire convulsions; fire and air and water burst forth...lightning and thunder crashed, and mountains and forests fell... And suddenly from the East a great brilliance shone forth; and there in the cloud I saw the Son of Man....

She also warned of the Antichrist. Her writings enjoyed a wide influence.

1186. In "The Letter of Toledo" everyone was warned to hide in the caves and mountains because the world was about to be destroyed.

Joachim of Fiore

1194. A big name among those who prophesied the endtime is Joachim of Fiore (c. 1125–1202). After meditating on the book of Revelation he suddenly saw harmony between the Old and New Testaments and history as developing in three ages, each one corresponding to a person of the Trinity. He predicted, in line with Montanus mentioned above, that the last stage of the world would be the 1000-year reign of the Holy Spirit, and that it would begin in 1260. But more than anyone else, he brought into mainstream apocalyptic thinking the notion that this reign, this golden age, would occur not at the end of history, as was previously held, but actually within history.

This idea has led, beyond Joachim's intent, to the connection between apocalyptic change and political reconstruction; that is, to future groups such as the Third Reich (third kingdom), Communism, British economic nationalism, and American confidence in "progress," each implying that theirs was the utopian kingdom here on earth predicted by this prophet. This notion would be further entrenched by the eighteenth-century Enlightenment, which definitively shifted responsibility for the future away from any heavenly influence to man's own efforts on earth. Progress was the key word, progress meaning man's construction of the New Jerusalem.

Joachim's influence on later medieval thought was enormous (a whole radical branch of so-called Spiritual Franciscans produced a rash of pseudo-Joachim writings). His ideas spawned the Apostolic Brethren (one of the first "Doomsday cults," in 1260), who were the first to take their apocalyptic ideas and turn them into armed resistance to the forces of church and state. To this extent they became the direct forebears of the tragic Waco incident seven hundred years later in 1993.

Joachim was encouraged by three successive popes. But

he did reintroduce millennarianism which previously had been rejected, and so, in 1215, the Fourth Lateran Council condemned his views on the Trinity.

1348. During the terrible Black Death warnings, self-flagellatists and others preached endtime prophecies.

1420. The Taborites were a radical sect in Bohemia led by defrocked priests; they came into being after the execution of John Hus in 1415. This group predicted that every city would be annihilated by fire and that only five mountain strongholds would be saved when Christ came between February 10th and 14th, 1420. When Christ failed to appear, they declared that in fact he did come but secretly (a stance adopted by the Jehovah's Witnesses when their predicted 1914 appearance also failed). From a certain pacifism they changed into a bloodthirsty military unit (the army of Christ, as they saw themselves, destined to execute the plagues of vengeance), until they were annihilated by a Bohemian army.

Savonarola

Savonarola (1452-1498) was a Dominican visionary who attracted large crowds with his prophecies of the Antichrist. Because it was near half-century time, he was only one of many in Italy going around preaching destruction. But he went further. Convinced that the French king, Charles VIII, was the "Second Charlemagne," he persuaded the people to submit to him peacefully. They did. They cast out the Medici rulers and became a kind of messianic republic (for three years). Florence, in Savonarola's view, was the new center, the seat of a reformed papacy, the New Jerusalem replacing Rome; all this implied that Rome was the Antichrist. As a result of this teaching he was excommunicated by the corrupt pope, Alexander VI. His fate was sealed by this papal opposition, the loss of support, and the collapse of Charles VIII's army. Savonarola was publicly executed in May of

1498. His "contribution," if you will, lay in giving Florence a sense of moral superiority and international influence to which all would submit. This laid the foundation, in another era, for that sense of "manifest destiny" which surfaced in England and America.

Nostradamus

1523. Another high profile name is Nostradamus (real name, Michel de Notredame). His image still appears on the front page of today's tabloids. Born in France of Jewish parents (his family converted two years before his birth) he became a physician and moved to Salon in 1544. There he gained a reputation for his innovative medical treatments during an outbreak of a plague. Around 1547, he began making his prophecies which he published in rhymed quatrains. Some of his prophecies appeared to be fulfilled, and his fame became so great that he was invited to the court of Catherine de Medici, where he cast horoscopes.

Before he died in 1566, Nostradamus burned his life's work, leaving behind his little four-line rhymed prophecies called "Centuries," written in the shadow of the Inquisition, in a mixture of archaic French, Latin, Greek, Italian, and English. In a word, they were written in code—a code which, according to his translators, foresaw cars, planes, Hitler, moon landings, and alien visitors. His prophecies were condemned by the Catholic church in 1781, but he continues to fascinate and influence endtimers and their prophecies. He has been interpreted to predict, for example, that the present pope will be assassinated while traveling, and that the last pope will be the tool of the Antichrist who will take over Italy and Greece, destroy Rome, and cause a worldwide drought that will start in Italy.

Actually, Nostradamus achieved his current fame largely through the translations of the late English medieval scholar, Erika Cheetham, who wrote such bestsellers as *The Prophecies of Nostradamus* and *The Final Prophecies of Nostradamus*, in which latter book she claimed to have found predictions of the Apollo 13 catastrophe and the spread of AIDS. In her skeptical moments, however, she confessed, "It's all rubbish, you know. Some of it is so vague and tortured and you could bend all sorts of events to fit it." People have bent it and still do; since the 1990s, at least ten Nostradamus titles have appeared in print, and when the Persian Gulf War broke out, sales tripled. A good example of such bending is his being credited with predicting the outbreak of Armageddon in 1999. He predicted no such thing. What he actually wrote was that his work "is comprised of prophecies from today to the year 3797." Some enterprising person, producing a page of impenetrable arithmetic, "proved" that when Nostradamus wrote 3797 he really meant 1999. This kind of forced projection is almost standard in all such endtime predictions.

Muntzer and Bockelson

1524. The most notorious prediction was made by the half-mad Thomas Muntzer who predicted the imminent coming of Christ after he led the peasants in a slaughter against the nobles. Moreover, the Lord had told him he would catch in his sleeves any cannon balls shot by the enemy. He was mowed down.

But it was in the city of Munster that fanaticism reached its logical conclusion. Rejecting both Catholicism and Lutheranism, many people chose to join the Anabaptists, a loose collection of apocalyptic sects. Munster announced that it was to become the New Jerusalem. Led by one Jan Bockelson he began his rule by running naked through the town, moved quickly from Puritanism to sexual license, reinstituted polygamy, declared himself King and Messiah of the Last Days, and conducted mass beheadings in the town square. Dressed in robes and surrounded by his teenage wives, he declared that the Second Coming would occur only when all priests, monks, and rulers were killed. Munster was eventually besieged and the inhabitants put to death. (The frightful episode of Munster resonates in Waco where David Koresh claimed sexual privileges and declared himself the endtime messiah.)

We should note here that Muntzer, Bockelson, and others are the perfect example of an idea gone wild, the idea being the Protestant Reformation's ideal that each person could read and interpret the Bible (now available in the vernacular) for himself/herself. This opened the floodgates of amateur prophecy. (This virus is still with us in the endless rantings of amateur endtimers, as a casual look at the Internet will show.) Once the Reformation denied the church's authority in interpreting the Bible, once the "plain" reading of Everyman replaced tradition, it was impossible to maintain control of speculation about the end of the world and of idiosyncratic readings of the books of Daniel and Revelation. (An aversion to the multiplicity of interpretations and the need for a central authority of tradition is almost always behind the conversion of evangelical ministers to Catholicism.) By destroying devotional works, the priesthood, art, and the monasteries which used to point people heavenward as it were, the Reformation unwittingly left the world as the only arena of activity and salvation, thus giving rise to a millennial view of history: the New Jerusalem will be established here.

Moving Forward to 2000

1568. One of the more famous predictions was made by Archbishop James Ussher who predicted that the world would end in the fall of 1996.

1809. A certain Mary Batement claimed she had a magic chicken that laid eggs with endtime messages on them, one of which said that Christ was coming. She caused much panic until someone discovered she was forcing an egg into a chicken! She was eventually hanged for poisoning someone.

1843. Another famous case is that of William Miller who founded Millerism. Originally a Baptist convert, he determined from his biblical calculations that the Second Coming would happen around 1843. Thousands followed his teaching and began to prepare for Christ's return. 1843 came and went, so Miller specified the new date as March 21, 1844, and then October 22, 1844. His movement was down but not out when nothing materialized (it was called The Great Disappointment). Seventh Day Adventists and Southern Baptists have held on to some of the millennium concepts.

1910. The return of Halley's comet was, as might be expected, a sign for many of the Second Coming.

1914. Charles Russell founded the Jehovah's Witnesses, and said that Jesus would return in 1914. The Jehovahs, holding the record for failed predictions, went on to add 1918, 1925, 1941, 1975, 1984, and 1994. They finally threw in the towel and got out of the prediction business.

1953. A man named David Davidson wrote a book entitled, *The Great Pyramid, Its Divine Message*, and predicted that the world would end in 1953.

1988. The book, *88 Reasons Why the Rapture Is in 1988*, came out and, when that didn't pan out, guess what? A new book entitled: *88 Reasons Why the Rapture Is in 1989*.

1993. Some may recall that in the 1990s, David Koresh of the Branch Davidians in Waco, Texas, taught that the final battle of Armageddon would start at his compound, and that the world would end in 1995. Tragically, after a 51-day standoff with federal authorities, on April 10, 1993, seventy-six members died in a fire.

1995. On March 20th the apocalyptic sect in Japan, the Aum

Shinriko, released poison gas on a Japanese subway, hospitalizing some 5,500 people and killing twelve of them. Its megalomaniac leader, Shoko Asahara, the typical authoritarian leader with messianic pretensions and dressed in a purple robe, had attracted a large number of young scientists. He brainwashed them and, following his interpretation of the book of Revelation, predicted that Armageddon would occur by the year 2000; Asahara claimed that he was hastening it by using the poison gas.

1997. Sun Magazine reported that Noah's Ark had been found, containing six copper, gold, and silver scrolls which revealed that doomsday is set for the year 2001.

1997. The tragedy of the Heaven's Gate cult whose members committed mass suicide. They determined that the Hale-Bopp comet would eject a space capsule containing lethal "pathogens," and all life on earth would die.

1998. Under its leader, Heng-ming Chen, a Taiwanese cult operating out of Garland, Texas (he picked Garland because it sounded closest to "God-land"), predicted not only that Christ would return precisely on March 31, 1998, but that he would appear on channel 18 on television. He didn't.

1998. A group called Centro, a very active organization centered in the Philippines, predicts the world will come to an end in 1998.

1998. Michael Drosnin, author of the popular book, *The Bible Code*, claims to have found a hidden message in the first five books of the Bible (the Pentateuch). He predicts that World War III will start either in 2000 or 2006.

2000. Looking to the future, on May 5th in the year 2000, all the planets are supposed to be in alignment; this supposedly will cause earthquakes and other disasters which are, for some, the biblical signs preceding the Second Coming.

Other Traditions

As we might expect, these are mostly Christian (failed) predictions since the Second Coming referred to is, of course, that of Christ; the Christian Scriptures speak freely of it. However, we should be aware that other traditions and religions have their versions of the endtime. Buddhism sees the world running in a circular pattern and therefore there is really no end to it. Still, there is a notion among Buddhists that both Buddhism and our age are coming to an end. Among the Jews, the endtime is seen in the coming of the Messiah. In 1991, for instance, Manachem Schneerson, a Russian-born rabbi, foresaw that the Messiah would come by September 9, 1991, the start of the Jewish New Year. Then there is the incident of the Red Cow. In the 19th chapter of the book of Numbers, which describes ritual cleansing using the ashes of a slaughtered red heifer, it says, "A red heifer without defect, in which there is no blemish and on which no yoke has been laid." Well, Melody is a red heifer born on a farm in northern Israel in 1997. Some rabbis claim Melody is the first red heifer born in Israel in 2000 years, and therefore, they speculate, could she be the harbinger of the Messiah?

How these people and scores of others calculate with such certainty the end of the world or Christ's Second Coming is lost, for most of us, in the convoluted, labyrinthine language and thought processes of the calculators and in an over-familiarity with the exotic books of the Bible and other esoteric readings. And, like computers, endtime language is something all its own, with its own esoteric vocabulary.

Endtime Glossary

Here's a quick glossary for those of you who may be interested.

The AntiChrist. Anybody who is currently the embodiment of evil. The front-running contender has been the pope, the perennial favorite since the days of Luther. Luther insisted that the document from Pope Leo X which excommunicated him could only have come from the Antichrist, and he later explicitly identified the pope as such. In this he was followed by John Calvin, Zwingli, Knox, and many members of Protestant England. Then the honor passed to Mohammed, Oliver Cromwell, the Huns, Saracens, and Turks, who were wreaking havoc in the middle ages, to Napoleon and Saddam Hussein—in short, to whomever fit the description. In our own history the Antichrist was identified with Hitler (see below) and Mussolini. At times people actually longed for the Antichrist since, in the logic of apocalypticism, its coming presaged the eventual triumph of Christ (an example: the thrill of the Jehovah's Witnesses at the outbreak of World War I).

The Beast. This character appears in the book of Revelation and seems to be a world leader who will orchestrate rebellion against God. Its occasional identification with the Antichrist is based on the totally non-related first epistle of John (2:18). The "mark of the beast" is seen by some to be the bar code on the products we buy or a computer chip to be inserted into us, all as a means for the Antichrist to control us.

666. The mark of the beast is 666, a number which has given rise to all kinds of fanciful interpretations. Some customers will not accept change that totals $6.66, and people will not accept license plates with those numbers. Hitler was considered the Antichrist because the letters of his name add up to 666; Gorbachev because in Russian, Mikhail S. Gorbachev adds up to 1,322 or 666 x 2. How about this? The space program designed to promote global thinking and therefore global mind control had enlisted three astronauts—Lovell, Anders, and Borman—and each had six letter names: 666!

Henry Kissinger's name in Hebrew adds up to 111 (666 divided by 6); the names Ronald Wilson Reagan each have six letters: 666 (Reagan, of all people, who had the address of his house in California changed from 666 to 668). One enterprising pastor, with tongue in cheek, has proven that Barney the Dinosaur is the Antichrist. First, he says, you start with CUTE PURPLE DINOSAUR, then you convert all the U's to V's, which is the proper Latin anyway. You then extract all the Roman numerals, namely CV, VL and DIV, and convert them to Arabic values, which would be 100, 5, 5, 50, 500, 1, and 5. When you add them all up you get 666! Barney as the Antichrist? Why not? This pastor's interpretation makes as much sense as the others.

The Rapture (from the Latin meaning "snatched away" from which we derive the words robbery and rape). Faithful Christians who profess the Lord Jesus will be snatched away as the terrible destruction rains down on the earth and destroys the rest of humankind. Of course, those destroyed comprise the majority of humanity since, statistically, a very small portion of the human race has accepted Jesus Christ as its personal savior.

The Tribulation. This follows (or precedes, depending on what endtime scenario you hold; see below) the rapture. It is a seven-year time period of chaos, war, plagues, etc.

Armageddon. This refers to the final showdown, as in the old cowboy movies. It's the final battle between Good and Evil and it will take place, according to the book of Revelation (16:16 and 19:19–21), in the valley of Megiddo, a small valley in Israel. This will be quite a feat, since that valley is no bigger than a football field or two.

The Millennium. The word means "thousand" and refers to the thousand-year imprisonment of Satan and the earthly rule of Christ. It's based on a strictly literal interpretation of the book of Revelation (20:1–15) which says that Satan will be chained for a thousand years, and the martyrs and those faithful to Jesus will come to life (the first resurrection), and for 1000 years share Christ's kingdom. When the 1000 years end, Satan will be permitted to resume his activity, but, after a bitter struggle, he will be definitively overcome in the Last Judgment. The faithful will go to heaven (second resurrection) and the unfaithful will go to hell (second death).

Eschatology. The beginning of the end. This is followed by the Final Judgment.

There are different scenarios in the arrangement of all this. You have the Pre-tribulation or Premillenium which says the rapture will come before the Great Tribulation so that the chosen may be spared all the chaos. Then there is Post-Tribulation or Postmillennium which says no, the rapture will come after the middle of the Tribulation, which means that some of the chosen will have to suffer like everybody else. Then there's the version which claims that we're already living in the millennium, which is the age of the church, and that things will get better and better until Christianity becomes dominant so as to herald the Second Coming of Christ. Finally there's a scenario called Preterism which says that the prophecies of Jesus have, in fact, already been fulfilled in the destruction of Jerusalem in the year 70 of this era. What these scenarios all have in common is a timetable.

6

The Persistent Teaching

Gather ye rosebuds while ye may,
Old Time is still a-flying,
And this same flower that smiles today,
Tomorrow will be dying.
—Robert Herrick

Some of you may remember Maxwell Smart. He was the character on television played by Don Adams. Smart was a spy at the height of the Cold War, working for an organization called Control whose purpose was to defeat the powers of evil. He was a bumbling sort of an agent, resorting to an odd grab bag of tricks to foil his enemies. He was given to hilarious exaggerations which forced him continually to revise his statements until they were more in touch with reality. For example: "You'd better drop that gun because this yacht happens to be surrounded by the Seventh Fleet. Would you believe the Sixth Fleet? How about a school of angry flounder?" Or, "As soon as you're gone, by the use of sheer brute strength I shall be able to rip these chains from the wall in one minute. Two minutes? How about a week from Tuesday?"

Maxwell Smart reminds me of the endtime calendar-setters who, without the slightest hint of embarrassment, keep revising their exaggerations and predict dates for the end of the world. Currently, according to the editor of *The*

Millennial Prophecy Report, there are over 350 organizations in the United States alone predicting some form of Armageddon as the last day of 1999 fades.

Inventive and Ingenious

How do they do it? Except for a few examples, we will not discuss the torturous use people make of Scripture and non-scriptural writings to come up with their predictions. Many are as inventive and ingenious as they are bizarre. One writer, for example, says that Ezekiel predicted the return of Christ. In 29:17 and 21, the prophet writes: "In the first month, in the first day of the month... In that day will I cause the horn of the house of Israel to bud forth, and I will give thee the opening of the mouth in the midst of them and they shall know that I am the Lord." It's clear to that writer, if to no one else, that with these words Ezekiel predicted both the month and day of the return of Christ. On the first day of the first month the "opening of the mouth," that is, the Word (remember John, chapter 1: "the Word was God and was made flesh and dwelt among us") will arrive.

Try this one. This same author quotes the saying of Jesus, "Now learn a parable of the fig tree: when its branch is yet tender and putteth forth leaves, ye know that summer is nigh. So likewise when ye shall see all these things, know that it is near, even at the doors." (He chose to use the old King James version). His interpretation? "When its branch is tender" means Israel is tender. Israel was born in 1948. The Six Day War was in 1967, making Israel 19 years old at the time, the age for "tenderness." "Summer is nigh" refers to June 5th, the beginning of the War. When all this happens, namely young Israel founded in 1948 + 19 (her tender age at war) equals 1967, the time of the war plus one forty-year generation equals 2007, the end of the age. So, the world will end in the year 2007, and it's all foretold in Scripture.

With the arrival of the atomic bomb and its potential for

worldwide destruction, preachers were ecstatic. Now the concept of worldwide destruction was not only the preserve of a few Bible believers. It was now a frightening possibility for everyone. The preachers went to work. Not only did they claim that nuclear bombs were foretold in Scripture but also that their eventual cataclysmic use offered an "exact picture" of the burning and melting depicted in 2 Peter 3:10. And in 2 Peter 3:10, it says, "Seeing then that all these things shall be dissolved"...dissolved meaning to unfasten or release, thereby foretelling nuclear fission. (Why not?)

One preacher believed that God destroyed Sodom and Gomorrah with nuclear power. Another claimed that atomic energy was in the Bible all along, and he quoted Zechariah, "For who hath despised the day of small things?" [i.e. the atom] (Zechariah 4:10). All the acts of devastation in the prophetic books were interpreted as the fallout from a nuclear blast. In fact, the prophets had foretold that nuclear blasts were the precise means the Lord would use to end the world.

Hal Lindsey's *The Late Great Plant Earth* was practically a manual of atomic-age combat. Zechariah's image of human flesh being consumed portrays "exactly what happens to those who are in a thermonuclear blast"; "fire and brimstone" equal tactical nuclear weapons; "falling stars" equal warheads or intercontinental missiles; "stinging locusts" equal helicopters; the "scorching heat" of the book of Revelation equals radiation, and on and on. Others went even further. Jeremiah's "make bright arrows" equals the launching of nuclear missiles; Habakkuk's "for they shall heap dust and take it" equals radioactive fallout; and Ezekiel's seven-month delay in burying the dead is for the necessary cooling-off period due to the radioactive contamination of the corpses.

The Inevitable End

Jerry Falwell offered a whole series of predictions about the inevitable end of the world, from God-ordained nuclear war to the final holocaust following Russia's invasion of Israel. Pat Robertson predicted the ultimate holocaust by 1982; he pulled back not only because 1982 came and went, but also because he had his eye on the White House. Billy Graham also embraced prophecy. "Secular history is doomed," he wrote in his 1965 book, *World Aflame.* History's final movements, he wrote in his 1983 *Approaching Hoofbeats* (referring to the four horsemen of the book of Revelation) were "perhaps just ahead." And, of course, former President Ronald Reagan was very much interested in prophecy. At the now famous 1971 dinner with California legislators, he offered a chain of evidence that "for the first time ever, everything is in place for the battle of Armageddon and the Second Coming of Christ."

It is, of course, the year 2000 that has galvanized the conservative evangelicals most. This date is the driving force behind their incredible mission to convert the world before it's too late. Since the founding of the state of Israel in 1948, and the development of nuclear weapons and their spread (India and Pakistan being the latest nuclear nations), they believe that we are clearly living in the endtime. Their bookstores are overflowing with endtime titles. Missionary activity is at an all-time high, for they must gather as many souls to Christ as possible before time runs out. After all, did not Jesus clearly say, "And the good news of the kingdom will be proclaimed throughout the world, as a testimony to the nations; and then the end will come" (Matthew 24:14)? Besides, their preaching is actually bringing about the endtime even with its terrifying tribulations. But, of course, they have nothing to fear for they will rise to meet Christ in the air. So they go forth with the word: accept Jesus Christ as your personal Savior.

The Israeli Connection

The evangelical prophecy people, as you might suspect, have an almost fanatical connection with the Jews. You see or read their uncritical and effusive support for the state of Israel at every turn. But that connection is profoundly ambiguous. Let me explain. First of all, the Jewish people necessarily loom large in prophecy. After all, it's their books and their prophets that the evangelicals cite. For them (unlike Catholics) the Jews play a major role in the endtime scenario. Initially the Jew was the classic Antichrist in the medieval mystery plays. People like Joachim of Fiore (we've met him earlier) argued that while all Jews will eventually be converted, before they are, they will follow the Antichrist and cause much harm. From this understanding the Jew soon became the Antichrist and the seeds for anti-Semitism were sown.

But, to condense a lot of history, the dominant motif that ultimately emerged was that, according to Scripture prophecy, the Jews were to be returned to their land, there establish a nation, and undergo persecution. The survivors would hail Christ as Messiah who would come again, and that would be the end of the script. Some favorite prophecies included Jeremiah: "Behold, I will gather them out of all countries whither I have driven them in mine anger...and I will bring them again unto this place, and I will cause them to dwell safely"; and Isaiah: "And the Lord shall assemble the outcasts of Israel and gather together the dispersed of Judah from the four corners of the earth." In this way the restoration of the Jewish people to their homeland became a major endtime motif and a sign that the end was near. (Not all prophecy folk hold Israel to be a key, notably the Seventh Day Adventists and the Jehovah's Witnesses). In other words, the Jews must return to Palestine as a condition for the Second Coming.

Some argued that the Jews must be converted to Christ

first and then be restored as a nation; others held to the opposite view: nationhood first, then conversion. This latter prevailed and many evangelicals worked hard to support the Zionist movement. For them it had nothing to do with secular planning (founding father Theodore Herzl was a secular Jew), but everything to do with God's plan. So in 1937, when David Ben Gurion told the British Royal Commission on Palestine, "The Bible is our mandate," the prophecy people were ecstatic; when Israel was declared a nation on May 14, 1948, they were beside themselves. Surely, with this sign in place, Jesus would come at any moment. The Six Day War of 1967, and the recapture of the Old City of Jerusalem (clearly foretold by Zechariah, according to some evangelicals), only confirmed the expectation. It wasn't long before the date-setters were at it again, using Israel's nationhood as a starting point for calculations. The Rapture was near!

So, for the most part, the prophecy people—especially the premillennianists (those saying destruction first, the 1000-year reign later) gave unqualified if not fawning support for Israel. Apart from American Jews themselves, they became Israel's firmest backers and were politically influential on behalf of Israel's interests. As Jerry Falwell put it, "Theologically, any Christian has to support Israel, simply because Jesus said to." Hal Lindsey warned, "If the U.S. ever turns its back on Israel, we will no longer exist as a nation." Such support covered even Israel's expansionist policies, both legal and illegal, which, many evangelicals thought, should include the original boundaries of the Old Testament anyway: from "the river of Egypt unto the great river, the river Euphrates" (Genesis 15:18), which meant gobbling up most of the mideast.

Anti-Arab Bias

Such expansion also meant, of course, that the Arabs had to go, since God gave the land to the Jews. It was as simple as that. This attitude reflected a distinct anti-Arab bias among the evangelicals, a bias rooted in the medieval identification of Mohammed and Islam with the Antichrist or Gog. Anti-Arab bias especially colored much of the post-1948 writing. After all, if God is clearly on Israel's side, what point is there in trying to bring peace between Israel and the Arabs who are foreordained to "perpetual hatred," as one evangelical put it? These same backers of Israel naturally looked forward to the rebuilding of the Temple (the last thing the Israelis want! Who wants to go back to slaughtering all those cows?). Again, it didn't matter that the Arab Mosque of Omar was on the site of the old Temple. It, too, would have to go, by fair means or foul, for the restoration of the Temple was an absolute necessity for the completion of the prophetic picture. One prophecy writer, Salem Kirban, has the Antichrist zap the mosque with his ruby laser ring.

The Israelis themselves privately thought that the evangelicals were all a bit weird, running around with their arcane prophecies. However, they were shrewd enough to court their support, hosting their conferences and the like. As commentator Irving Kristol said in 1984, about a fundamentalist leader who claimed that God did not hear Jewish prayers, "Why should Jews care about the theology of a fundamentalist preacher...? What do such theological abstractions matter against the mundane fact that the same preacher is vigorously pro-Israel?" This policy paid off in positive publicity through the enormous networking of the pro-Israel evangelical tapes, books, seminars, and radio and television stations.

But as we said, the stand of the evangelicals regarding the Jews was ambiguous. There was, as we have seen, unqualified support for Israel as a necessary piece in the endtime puzzle. But, on the other hand, Jewish suffering for not accepting Jesus as the Messiah was also part of the puzzle. That is, before any glorious future for the Jews could be envisioned, they must first be punished for their sinfulness and must atone for "the murder of Christ." In this scheme of things, the Nazi holocaust (foretold, of course) was a regrettable but necessary part of history, a direct consequence of Jewish spiritual blindness. As popular prophecy writer Jack Van Impe put it, "The Jews missed their Messiah. He walked among them and they did not recognize him." Not only that, the Holocaust was but a preview of what the Antichrist will do to the Jews in the future. They must "drink of the cup of God's wrath" for their continuing failure to show "repentance and faith in Christ Jesus." Later on in 1976, there would finally be a denunciation of the Holocaust, but it was still considered a "part of Israel's sacred history."

The scenario runs somewhat along these lines: the Antichrist will trick the Jews into the rebuilding of the Temple, then demand to be set up there (as Daniel foretold). On the Jews who did not realize their mistake, there will be unleashed a horrible bloodbath; only a remnant will accept Jesus and be saved. (The usual ratio is that two-thirds of the Jews shall perish.) Hal Lindsey called it God's "disciplinary action." As another writer put it, "It took a Hitler to turn the Jews toward Palestine. It will take a greater Hitler (the Antichrist) to turn them to God." Fundamentalists might feel sympathy for all the suffering the Jews have undergone and will undergo, but what can be done? It's all foreordained, all right there in prophecy. Even the later soft-peddling, the desire to convert the Jews, would not hide a latent anti-Semitism and over-preoccupation with the Jewish people that still remains a fundamentalist legacy.

The New Age

> Put simply, the New Age is apocalyptic: it believes in an Endtime. This fact is not always immediately apparent, since the movement

tends to concentrate on the process of personal, individual transformation. But there is a sum to these parts, and it is nothing less than the salvation of the entire planet. Most New Agers have experienced some sort of personal transformation in their lives, and believe that if sufficient numbers of people follow their example the face of the earth will be transformed. There is, admittedly, no consensus about how the transformation will come about, or the shape of the world after it happens: vague phrases such as a "shift in consciousness" tend to obscure very different visions of the mechanics of change, which can involve beams of psychic energy, geographical cataclysms, reincarnated masters, extraterrestrial aliens, or, as Rabanne illustrates, all of the above. The crucial point, however, is that this new world, however it is constituted and however long it is supposed to endure, represents the sum of human history.

This quotation from Damien Thompson refers back to chapter one, where we wrote that we would save our comments concerning the New Age and apocalypticism for the wider context of this present chapter. In a nutshell, the New Age is definitely classic apocalypticism. Some New Agers hold the theory of a "parallel planet" that is coming our way. When it is close enough, they say, people can jump aboard and journey to a new life in a new world. Or, according to New Age guru, Paco Rabanne, the New Age boasts the conviction that we are moving through a "preceding of the equinoxes," from the evil Age of Pisces to the golden Age of Aquarius, a millennium of wisdom and light after the year 2000.

The signs are all there: earthquakes, pollution, global warming. Sooner or later Gaia, the living organism of the earth, will take revenge. The Antichrist is at hand. In fact, he is a teenage American boy. But so is Maitreya, a messianic figure who, sponsored by the Terra Center, held a press conference in London. However, no one showed up so he is still waiting in the wings. But there is hope for the Elohim, extraterrestrial beings who created Atlantis and will rescue humanity just as they did Noah. If warnings are heeded, men and women will evolve into the "Fourth Vibratory Plane."

This kind of mumbo-jumbo inevitably spawns best-selling New Age books like, *You are Becoming a Galactic Human.* And no wonder thousands of New Agers gathered at "power centers" throughout the world on August 16, 1987, to celebrate the "Harmonic Convergence" of the Mayan and Hopi Indian calendars and the alignment of the planets. At these centers, especially the one in Seattle, they "vibrated" together in prayer in union with the universe. When nothing happened, they all went home. In short, for all of its nebulous and slippery identity, the one thing we can say about the New Age is that it definitely believes in the endtime and the transformation of the earth—minus divine punishment for the unsaved: nature itself will take care of that—and some vague "shifting and expanding of consciousness," depicting the apex of human history with no more poverty, starvation, or mistakes of the past, a world where people can tap directly into each other's minds. You can't get more apocalyptic than that.

The Catastrophe Scenario

The old catastrophe scenario was given a boost by Ruth Montgomery (often called the mother of the New Age) and Edgar Cayce, a big name in the New Age constellation. The latter was an American clairvoyant who died in 1945, and who literally wrote volumes. He rewrote history, claiming Atlantis was an advanced civilization destroyed in the biblical flood which left a few survivors. California and the east coast will disappear into the sea as a result of "earth changes," a shift in the earth's magnetic poles, and by the year 2000 a new world will appear. But not before a lot of destruction takes place.

The channeling practiced by the New Agers is first cousin to the aliens who regularly come in UFOs to abduct earthlings and deliver messages which foretell disaster for the earth unless humans mend their ways. Only the New Agers have ancient dead people deliver the message. Such channeling soon became a full-time industry and the source of many bestselling books like the popular *A Course in Miracles*.

Astrology also figures strongly in New Age because it lines up the earth's rotation through the twelve signs of the zodiac (the "preceding of the equinoxes") until the Age of Aquarius is reached. New Agers are also fascinated with pyramids which in some way reflect the passage of the sun through the signs of the zodiac. The pyramids, they contend, contain coded information about the date of the Second Coming.

You can sense that it's hard to pinpoint New Age teachings, which range from astrological fantasies to theories about Jewish conspiracies or about bankers taking over the world. Their teachings are constantly mutating, changing configuration as they prove false or useless or simply passé. They become more nebulous and less relevant as the years go on. The one constant is the vast outpouring and marketing of New Age products, from seminars, videos, correspondence courses, and artifacts, to books like the bestsellers *The Fingerprints of God*, the *Mayan Prophecies* and *The Celestine Prophecy*.

We should take note here that, although evangelicals are hostile to the New Age and resent some of its teachings, their ideas actually converge on many points. Again, as

Damien Thompson writes in his excellent book, *The End of Time:*

> Both movements began [in the 1980s] to pro-
> duce date-specific prophecies... Could it be that
> in some respects they are essentially the same
> sort of religion? For movements which despise
> each other, the degree of overlap between
> Pentecostalism and the New Age is remarkable.
> Both rely heavily on disembodied voices rather
> than visions: the medium channeling communi-
> cations from spirit guides and the born-again
> believers speaking prophecies in tongues
> resemble each other in method of transmission
> and sometimes in content of the message (the
> urgent need for mankind to mend its ways).
> Both movements stress health and healing since
> they regard physical health as a token of spiri-
> tual well-being; sudden contact with the sacred
> can result in the miraculous disappearance of
> "incurable"diseases and conditions.
>
> There is also a stress on material prosperity as a
> sign of blessing, though the more sophisticated
> practitioners in both fields tend to soft-pedal
> this approach. More importantly, both
> Pentecostalism and the New Age lay huge stress
> on individual experience of the spiritual, lead-
> ing to complete personal transformation; and
> this goes hand in hand with a certain "do it
> yourself" approach to organizational structure
> which is common to the strictest biblical literal-
> ists and to the most laid-back Californian New
> Agers.

It is not hard to relate these shared features to

developments in Western culture and society over the last few years. The obsession with healing and the replacement of established hierarchies with the sole authority of personal experience go hand in hand: they reflect the preoccupations of societies in which traditional social and religious structures have been failing or even disappearing. In the West, no institution or authority has remained unquestioned; very few occupations are secure in the way that they were fifty years ago. Yet for some, at least, society offers a range of choices—economic, cultural and spiritual—unthinkable before the 1980s. The populations of North America and Europe are torn between a new materialism and an intense yearning for the sacred; the result has been a significant increase in uncertainty and free-floating anxiety, from which the conversionist dramas of the Pentecostalists and the New Age offer an instant release. (pages 208-210)

Where Do Catholics Fit?

Where do Catholics fit in all of this? The answer is that an apocalyptic strand remains woven into a minority Catholic subculture and has always been present unofficially. Today, as in the past, it finds its most fervent expression in interpretation of the appearances of the Virgin Mary, whose apparitions always increase during times of crisis (the earliest recorded vision of Mary is that of third-century St. Gregory the Wonderworker.) And so, in traditionalist Catholic circles, from South America to Japan, there is mounting excitement over the many apparitions worldwide of the Blessed Virgin foretelling the collapse of evil and the triumph of the gospel.

Especially appealing for Catholic traditionalists are the Fatima prophecies. In the spring of 1917, as most Catholics know, three children, ages nine, eight, and six, claimed to have received visits from Mary, and they were shown visions of the future. Some advocates say that the three children each represent a third of mankind, one third, the spiritually dead (that's Francisco, age 8, who only saw the visions but didn't hear Mary speak, and who died first in 1919 of influenza; dying first equals the spiritually dead); the second third, the people stuck in organized human-made religions (that's Jacinta, who died in February, 1920, also from influenza, who saw and heard the visions but did not respond; non-response=the stuck); and the final third, those who respond with open minds and a new consciousness (Lucia who saw, heard, and responded—not for nothing does her name mean light—is still living).

Added to this outline is the existence of the "Third Secret of Fatima" which Lucia has entrusted to the Vatican, where it remains locked in a drawer. It has been read by all the popes since John XXIII, all of whom have decided not to reveal its contents because, in the mind of pessimistic Catholic traditionalists, it is too terrible to reveal, perhaps because it involves a nuclear Armageddon.

A New Pentecost

More in the mainstream is that Marian messages since 1970 (and the fall of communism, claimed to have been foretold at Fatima) have moved to a motif of hope, promising a New Pentecost. The Virgin's appearances at Medjugorie in Yugoslavia, with her less apocalyptic and less controversial messages, have been the scene of an ongoing attraction for many. Their message is that the twentieth century is indeed under the power of Satan but that his power will wane as the century comes to a close—a message remarkably similar to the purported visions of Leo XIII in the 1890s and Pius X in 1909.

Marian newsletters are replete with endtime scenarios. The thousands of messages differ, but they all contain a core call to repentance, the foretelling of great and terrible trials, and the recommendation to pray the rosary in order to avert disaster. The new *Catechism of the Catholic Church* says that before Christ's Second Coming, "the Church must pass through a final trial that will shake the faith of many believers. The persecution that accompanies her pilgrimage on earth will unveil the 'mystery of iniquity' in the form of a religious deception... The supreme religious deception is that of the Antichrist, a pseudo-messianism by which man glorifies himself in place of God and of his Messiah come in the flesh" (para. 675). Here it seems to foretell a period of tribulation—a theme echoed in many Marian appearances.

The appearances of the Blessed Virgin Mary around the world and her prophetic utterances are held as true by more Catholics than ever before, indicating in a way that, although apocalyptic belief has been officially discouraged by the church, it has come in through the back door of Marian devotions and reputed prophecies. An example of the latter is a flyer I just received in the mail advertising audio and video cassettes by a Franciscan. There are titles such as as "Prescriptions for the Endtimes"; "Dear Children, Time is Short!"; "The Sun Will Be Darkened"; and "Please Help Me To Win My Battle Against Satan"—all based on "locutions" from Mary.

Ralph Martin, president of Renewal Ministries, Inc., in Ann Arbor, Michigan, is the author of a book, *Jesus is Coming Soon: A Catholic Perspective on the Second Coming.* He declares that although some elements of the Marian movement are at times exaggerated, the movement itself is, nevertheless, "authentic and prophetic." Mary, he says "is actually trying to draw the human race's attention to the fact that sin does still make a difference and conversion is important and repentance is important, and that the human race is facing some kind of grave danger." Martin lists certain signs that may, in fact, indicate that Jesus is returning soon.

Like so many others, he points to the re-establishment of Israel as a nation in 1947; the Six Day War in 1967, which put Jerusalem under the control of the Jews for the first time in 2,000 years; the world's "turning away" in large numbers from the values of Christianity; and the increase in "unrestrained mockery of God and of all things Christian...[Christianity] really is a message of life and death and there really is a heaven, there really is a hell, and final judgment will certainly come, and we need to be living in friendship with Jesus in order to end up in heaven rather than hell" (*Our Sunday Visitor* interview, July 26, 1998).

Catholic Prophecies?

Remember too the Prophecies of St. Malachy which spoke of the last pope. In today's climate, the word is that there are only two more popes after Pope John Paul II, someone not adverse to prophetic themes. In his book, *Crossing the Threshold of Hope*, for example, he relates that the attempt on his life on May 13, 1981, was linked to the anniversary of Mary's first appearance at Fatima.

Then there are the rumors afloat that Pope John XXIII left a secret, dusty, leatherbound diary, found by a Vatican cleaning woman who was sorting though boxes in a storage room. In this diary the pope made predictions about events leading up to the year 2000: wars (namely, the Vietnam War), famine (Mary revealed this on September 23, 1961), natural disasters (Mary revealed this on March 6, 1961) and Doomsday, which will begin with the detonation of an atomic bomb in a major European city by a Libyan terrorist group. This last event will cause a six-month war that will result in the death of millions. The pope also reputedly foretold the assassination of John F. Kennedy (Mary revealed this to him on April 7, 1959), the unrest in the Middle East, and the fall of communism. He wrote about visions with Jesus in February 12, 1959, and in April of 1963, of heavenly visitors and flaming chariots of steel.

All this will take place for eight years. Those eight years, however, are to be followed by a time of love and harmony. Saviors will arrive on earth in chariots on June 5, 1995, and begin the task of cleanup and repair. They will share their advanced knowledge with us; as a result most diseases will be wiped out, so that the average life span will be 150. Best of all, a wondrous miracle will take place in the sky above New York City when, on December 25, 2000, millions will witness the appearance of the Messiah who will announce the beginning of a second paradise on earth.

What all this says is that apocalyptic expectations are not confined to the right-wing traditionalists only (defined as critics and opponents of Vatican II), but find acceptance among the vast numbers of conservative Catholics (defined as critics but not opponents of that council). Despite official centuries-old distancing from apocalypticism, it is alive and well in many parts of the church.

The Official Stance

If a notable subcult of Catholics is actively apocalyptic, the official stance of the Catholic church is something different. For the most part, mainstream Roman Catholics are not officially a part of the apocalyptic scene. Why? The answer is, in general, that as Christianity took hold in the early Roman empire, its millennianist strand faded. In one sense, since the church was no longer under siege and was, since Constantine, linked to imperial power, this church freed of crisis (remember, apocalypticism is crisis literature) had no need to cling to its apocalyptic phase. Besides, the chaos of charismatic apocalypticism is not compatible with a settled establishment concerned with law and order and its own institutional importance. The attitude of caution appeared early in the writings of such people as the great third-century theologian Origen, who discarded calendar millennialism by shifting the focus from the end of the world to the destiny of the individual who could grow spiritually even after death.

But it was St. Augustine, more than any other, who in his masterwork, *City of God*, rejected millennialism. Such was his authority and influence that his approach officially distanced Catholic thought from all literalist readings of prophecy and the millennium. Not that Augustine, like all of his contemporaries, was not convinced that the end of the world was near. He just held that before this could happen there had to be a universal preaching of Christianity, and no one knew how long that would take. "The gospel of the Kingdom will be proclaimed throughout the earth as a testimony to all nations; then the end will come," he wrote. But who knows when that will happen? Besides, there was no need to be preoccupied with Christ's return at the end for he had, in one sense, already come back in the church, a church, furthermore, extended into eternity as the church militant on earth, the church suffering among the departed in purgatory, and the church triumphant in heaven.

The Catholic attitude was finally sealed when in 431 A.D., the Council of Ephesus condemned millennialism and endtime speculation. The church added several more condemnations throughout the centuries, the latest being a condemnation in 1944, of even a mitigated form of millenarianism. The Catholic church never taught, for example, that the world would end in the year 1000 or even 2000, and so, despite individual Catholics or even popes who flirted with it, the church distanced itself from any official apocalyptic goings on. The church, in fact, was resolutely opposed to anything that smacked of apocalyptic fervor. Even in adopting and promoting the newly designated Anno Domini calendar, the church in effect was creating a measured future scenario, one that unfolds at an even pace in contrast to episodic and idiosyncratic apocalyptic times, which feed on uncertainty and are disruptive. To this day, official Catholic teaching is still based on St. Augustine: that although the reign of the saints has in some respects already begun, any reference to a thousand years is purely figurative.

Currently, for mainline Catholics there is the preparation for the millennium outlined by Pope John Paul II in his letter, *Tertio Millennio Adveniente*. In it the pope describes a three-year preparation: 1997, the year of Jesus, 1998, the year of the Spirit, and 1999, the year of the Father leading to the celebration of the year 2000. The celebration has been muted, however, for there is no sign of a Catholic revival and every sign of continuing decline. There is nowhere near the success and pizzazz of evangelical conservative Christianity, nothing in the Catholic camp to compare with their incredible spread on every continent and their message that the end is near.

The Great Non-Issue

Maybe Catholic enthusiasm for the millennium and the end-time is muted because, when you come right down to it, this whole issue of apocalypticism and end-of-the-world scripts carries a certain embarrassment for believers. This is evidenced by the indisputable fact that although the Second Coming of Christ is firmly and unalterably embedded in Scripture and tradition, in our catechisms, Mass canons, and creeds, it remains peripheral for most of us. When was the last time you heard a homily preached on eschatology? We really can't do without it—it's such a part of our heritage—but, it seems, we can't do with it either. The basis of our dilemma is threefold. First, after two thousand years, there is the obvious and observable fact that the world has not ended and Jesus has not come back. The record on predictions, as we have seen, is nothing short of dismal. How can such notions any longer be credible?

Secondly, it is scientifically difficult to speak of the end of the world when we now know that it is several billion years old, and that life may have appeared on it only billions of years after its creation. The world may last another five billion years before the death of our sun causes its collapse. For most of its existence, then, this world of ours was without any human beings, and there is every likelihood that we as a human race will perish long before the world does. How do you fit prophecies about the end of the world into a framework like that?

Finally, the old spatial theological language has lost its force for us. It spoke of Jesus coming "down" to earth, of Elijah going "up" to heaven, the damned going "below." Our experience is not of a static, three-tier universe like that, with down and up and below like the attic, living room, and basement of a house. Our universe is not like that. It's a vast, endless, timeless evolutionary flowing mix, with no up or down or center. These spatial concepts, redolent of endtime talk, don't resonate with us. Anyway, the whole notion of an imminent end is not terribly attractive to people who have it made, people earning degrees, working at the executive level with huge salaries and perks who, if and when they go to church, are looking for messages about their personal lives and not some new worry about an approaching apocalypse. And clergy, too, belonging to a long-established tradition and always planning ahead for expansion, are not emotionally wed to a sudden return of Christ, no matter what their Scriptures say.

Still, eschatology is such an authentic and integral part of the Bible and tradition that we can't ignore it altogether. So, what do we do, how do we handle it? Reginald Stackhouse in his book, *The End of the World: A New Look at an Old*

Belief, describes three approaches people have taken to this dilemma. One is millennialism which we have seen: these are the folk who do take the Second Coming seriously and literally and who, in spite of two thousand years of "Melton's law" operating, claim a vast following to this day.

Another approach he calls the pastoral one. This is the one most churches, including the Catholic church, have adopted. Its focus is not on what's to come, but on the people here and now and how Christ has in fact already come into people's lives if they would but believe and see him. Grace is hidden everywhere. The Spirit lurks you know not where. Especially in the eucharist do we have Christ come again. The third approach is the social interpretation which finds Christ's coming in the destruction of unjust social systems which oppress the poor and marginal, a destruction which will make way for a new order. This is liberation theology. Thus we live uneasily with a major Christian tenet.

In the Mainstream

With the huge evangelizing successes of fundamentalist Christianity and its increased clout in politics and entertainment, it has moved more and more into mainstream America, bringing with it its apocalyptic messages. There is no doubt that, to the mind of its adherents, the Second Coming is coming quickly, giving evangelical Christians, spurred by the fascination of the year 2000, not only a special urgency in seeking converts but also a certain touch of paranoia as they continue to scare people by hectoring timetables, giving graphic descriptions of the endtime, naming the current Antichrist, and detecting global conspiracies run by something called "The Order of Illuminati" (Pat Robertson's phrase). The "Order" used to be communism, but since its fall the mantle of the "Evil Empire" has fallen on international bankers, the freemasons, the Jews, Catholics, the government—whomever. Being quintessentially the American outsiders, they see themselves in confrontation with Satan, a confrontation which they are convinced will begin in their lifetimes (hence their support of the gun lobby and militia movements).

We should remember once more that such a mentality appears throughout history. It always occurs when the familiar order is threatened, when ancient spiritual monopolies have broken down, and social structures have collapsed; indeed, we are witnessing that daily. It's what Mark Kingwell, author of *Dreams of Millennium: Report from a Culture on the Brink*, calls "a latent virus in the cultural body." Distrust of government; a marketplace media; glorified graphic violence; dizzying scientific, medical, and cultural changes; global warming; pollution; the breakdown of the family and the promotion of "lifestyles"; widespread divorce; a failed educational system; AIDS; the loss of common values and the glue of religion; the fracturing of society; one-third of the country's children born out of wedlock; a permanent drug culture; mainstream soft and hard pornography protected by law; children killing children; human embryos for sale; a skewed economic system which rewards ball players, rock stars, and CEOs with huge salaries—at last count there were 170 billionaires in America (compared to 13 in 1982); the widening gap between the rich and the poor; and a vulnerable workforce thrown off course by computer technology. This long litany provides a key to the discontent and frustrations of the average American and is explosive fodder for the apocalyptic mentality.

People Become Disoriented

The fact is that when you have breakdowns of traditional structures such as we are witnessing, people do become disoriented. When you come to the end of an era, as in the year 1999, hope grows that perhaps at last things will settle down, the old evils will be overcome, and a new world order will be in place next year. Apocalypticism offers the promise of precisely such a change, indeed a miraculous change, and a radical change at that. That is its appeal—an understandable appeal for anyone who feels powerless and embattled, anyone who has thrown up his or her hands in frustration crying, "Can things get any worse?" as they watch on TV the latest episode of a child wielding an Uzi machine gun, mowing down his classmates; or catch their own child watching hard core pornography on the Internet.

The apocalyptic promise, backed up by Scripture, is that the enemy will be vanquished, the battle will be fought, and, though terrible, will be won; evil will be punished and the good, decent folks will be rewarded. Even those who do not believe in Scripture, like UFO abductees, tend to be hopeful because, as they say, the "space brothers" will come and save us all and take us to a new level of evolution. The apocalyptic appeal is that it offers such a scenario and one that will occur soon; the feeling is that we have messed up so much on this planet (politically, environmentally, and morally) that our problems can only be solved by other-worldly intervention, from the outside.

Its genius is that it does address human concerns (far better than the liberal intellectuals) and people under pressure, under stress, resonate with the vivid images of warfare, punishment, and reward. Its genius is that it offers a social structure in place of society's social fragmentation, cohesion in place of rampant "diversity," a central source of authority and "answers": the Bible, a transcendent God in place of or at least along side of the current, user-friendly immanent God, and an expectation of the endtime tailored to the experiences of the individual. It does focus people, no doubt about that, and it gives them a certain amount of energy and the notion that history is not meaningless, as agnostic professors preach, but is going somewhere. The future is in the hands of God. There is a goal. And, then too, apocalypticism provides people with some magnificent language and vivid rhetoric that they can use in their everyday lives, language that lets them fantasize how their enemies will get it in the neck someday while they, the lowly, "will be lifted up."

God Is In Charge

Thus evangelical fundamentalists and their apocalyptic messages have the virtue of putting human life and human experience and human history into the context of faith. There is, as I wrote before, a plan. God is in charge. We are going somewhere. Justice will triumph. Life has ultimate meaning. Even though we're a speck in the endless cosmos, we're a special, privileged, and beloved speck awaiting redemption and the fullness of the Rapture. God is sovereign. Without any help from us, God will intervene and "make all things new again." In the last analysis, the apocalyptic mentality is a coherent and hopeful one, which may account for its persistence among its adherents, for their refusal to give up in spite of a record of failed prophecies, and for their confidence in their faith in the Second Coming and their courage as they face the future. Their millennialism has throughout history challenged the status quo and held that history is not static but dynamic, with the Lord of all guiding it to an end.

Even their doomsdaying, however, has an increasingly horrifying relevance to it. On July 15, 1998, a bipartisan panel of defense strategists released a unanimous report that a ballistic missile threat is not ten or fifteen years away, but much, much closer as Iran, North Korea, and other hostile nations are now able to "acquire the means to strike the U.S. within about five years of a decision." Enemies of the United States are now able to build such weapons, armed with biological or nuclear warheads, and launch them with a new means of delivery that can shorten the warning time to zero. To this extent, snicker as we might at the excesses and juvenile prophecies of some of the apocalyptic prophets and their Steven Spielberg type of endtime catastrophes, believers in Christianity owe them a debt for challenging Christian beliefs in the biblical word and their reliance on God in whose hands "all things live and subsist." It's not for nothing that the last word in the Bible is "Maranatha! Come, Lord Jesus!"

On the Other Hand

There are serious flaws in much of the apocalyptic pronouncements and activities, and the Catholic tendency to distance itself from apocalypticism has proven sound. Patricia Hunt, writing in *The Christian Century*, is right to warn her students: "Playing with apocalypticism is 'playing with fire.'" Much of the evangelical literature is truly petty and narrow. Sometimes the authors seem positively gleeful at the idea of annihilation threatening the majority of the world's people, smugly certain that they will be raptured into safety while others burn. They are weak on social justice—why bother redressing ills when they're part of the endtime scenario? Their elaborate scriptural arithmetic, as we have seen, borders on the ridiculous and absurd. Remember: even Barney can become the Antichrist.

They consistently come under "Melton's law" but move on to the next failed prediction without batting an eye. They remind me of Robert Schuller's story about the father who bragged to his son about what a great hunter he was. The son joined his father on the next hunting trip to see for himself. They sat in the duck blind for a time until one lonely waterfowl winged its way through the sky. The father took aim, fired, and missed. "Son," he said, "you have just witnessed a miracle. There flies a dead duck."

Apocalypticism draws more than its share of the disturbed and megalomaniacs, as we have seen in our time with the poisoning in Japan, the Hale-Bopp comet fiasco, and the

Waco debacle. People who like to tinker with esoteric codes, who delight in arcane teasings from apocryphal or canonical books, people who fill the Internet with fanaticism or arm themselves in survivalist camps—all are victims and purveyors of a false religion. Even mainstream preachers like Jerry Falwell and Pat Robertson; other fevered evangelical ministers waving their Bibles at TV audiences; and the prolific authors of bestselling endtime books, all whip up a sound and fury that, in the last analysis, are as baseless and unstable as their constantly mutating scenarios, intended to fit the next crisis that comes along.

We might well ponder the cautious words of Alexander DiLella in his book, *Daniel:*

> At the outset, I must emphasize that Daniel does not speak of our times, but rather to our times. The book does not provide a forecast of the future but a pattern or example of how God had entered into the history of the original readers on the one hand and, on the other, how this same God wills that you be involved in the lives of believers today....

> Because of the turbulent times in which we live, many people are fascinated by the apocalyptic literature of the Bible. The peculiar imagery found in such books as Revelation and Daniel, especially the apocalyptic visions in chapters 2 and 7-12, seems to fuel the religious imagination. Those not acquainted with the methods of modern biblical studies may fancy that they can find in these books more or less clear allusions to political, military, and social upheavals happening in our time, or even see predictions of the future outcome of history. Such people even look to the apocalyptic literature of the Bible for

solutions to complex problems facing our society today. Because the homiletic stories in Daniel 1-6 and 13-14 tell of divine interventions to rescue the faithful Jews, some people today believe that God will again intervene dramatically and perhaps spectacularly in human affairs. It will be only a matter of time. As we approach the turn of the millennium we can expect even more speculations of this kind.

At the outset, we should lay to rest any interpretation that sees in the apocalypses of Daniel ancient predictions of the actual times in which we live, or even timetables of the Endtime, which some Christians imagine will occur in the not too distant future.

Nor should we hope to find in the homiletic stories clear solutions to social, political, and moral problems of great complexity. If we accept Daniel on its terms and not on ours, then it has much more to offer than the often simple-minded solutions of misguided interpreters. The authors of the various parts of the book had a profound faith and hope in the God of revelation, who is Lord of history. They address the book to believers—ancient and modern—who share that faith and hope. (*Daniel*, pp. 14-15, New City Press, 1997)

What Is the Answer?

So, what should be our stance? First of all, it's hard to duck apocalyptic themes as the new millennium approaches, especially as Hollywood, which always taps the popular pulse, steps up its production of endtime horror movies such as *Deep Impact* (meteor hitting the earth) or *Armageddon* ("On July 1st, School's Out...Forever."). Concerning this latter film, *New York Times'* movie critic, Janet Maslin, is on target:

> Doom threatens. *Again.* This time it's a giant asteroid ("It's the size of Texas, Mr. President"), and it's the Chrysler Building that becomes New York's most conspicuously flattened landmark (just as *Deep Impact* toppled the Statue of Liberty and *Godzilla* wrecked the Brooklyn Bridge.) That damage is done by a fake meteor shower during the first part of *Armageddon*. The sight, however apocalyptic, isn't as scary as the prospect of raising a generation of Americans on movies like this. (July 1, 1998)

Nevertheless, even as the year 2000 comes and goes (and the megaphones of apocalyptic warnings will continue to sound a good ten years after that date) we should forthrightly reject all these scare tactics and all those TV preachers and endtime books (including Catholic ones), especially those which disturb us, which offer us more the products of fertile imaginations than reality, even if current scenarios seem to fit so well and so cogently into the wild symbols of the books of Daniel or Revelation. Remember you can make anything sound plausible, but also remember Melton's Law.

Secondly, remember that Jesus said, "No one knows either the day or the hour," but only the heavenly Father. Sooner or later, of course, someday in a distant future, the end will come but no one will be around to cheer. Stick with the Catholic tradition whose note is hope not destruction and whose slide into a new millennium is one of promise and jubilee. Hillel Schwartz, in his book *Century's End: An Orientation Toward the Year 2000*, suggests that we take the fear out of the threat people anticipate, and view the times rather as a treat, a challenge. We should look forward to conquering cancer, AIDS, and other diseases. It is up to us to determine whether the new millennium will be a time of anxiety or of increased hope. It is worthwhile to remember that the Bible is a forward-looking book understood best by people oriented toward the future and that the word apocalyptic does not mean something horrendous but something revealed, that "something" being the compassion of God in Christ.

Let us end with the words of the Cardinal Archbishop of Milan, Carlo Maria Martini, who brings us back to basics, not only for the year 2000, but for all the years that follow:

> Even though millions throughout the world do not accept the central place of Christ, they do recognize, nevertheless, that in a certain way a new time in history began with his birth. In short, everyone on this globe has some relationship to Jesus Christ and the implications of his doctrine—about universal peace, forgiveness, love of enemies, solidarity, and love for the poor. In this sense the Pope rightly says that this is an event that in some way concerns everybody...

> For some, changing the calendar year from 1999 to 2000 has little religious significance; but for believers such a change signals a desire to renew hope and courage according to the apocalyptic dimension of the Gospels. We should not expect some big change in human history as we celebrate the new millennium. The year 2001 will not offer significant differences, other than a chance to seek essentials, to listen to the voice of the Holy Spirit, to regain an awareness

of the great and essential change in human history brought forth by the coming of Jesus Christ. Yes, changes will occur, since we live daily in this change; every prayer well uttered is this change; every act of love is this change—all brought about by the life, death, and resurrection of Jesus. The meaning of things has been changed. Every moment, this present moment, brings with it the presence of a new humanity, and we can look at everything in a different way. We can work for justice and love with a certainty that justice and love shall prevail, assured that it is already in the present order of things. In the kingdom of God, the days of forgiveness and love have begun and this order shall be forever. God's glory shall be revealed day after day.

7

Collapse of the "Total Church"

The parish churches were like people's palaces...
like going to the big picture houses in town with
their deep carpets and chandeliers and the usherettes
in their nice dresses.

—An old parishioner

One of Gary Larson's great "Far Side" cartoons shows two old, toothless dogs sitting in their rockers on the front porch; the mail has just been delivered by a cat who is leaving with the mailbag over his shoulder. The caption reads, "We're getting old, Zeke." Which means, of course, in younger days, that cat would be in fear of its life.

That cartoon leads to our topic: in younger days, the church would have dealt easily enough with the "far side" tenets of the New Age and fundamentalism and endtime scenarios. Now, like the old dogs on the porch, it is somewhat toothless and defenseless against such onslaughts. Its position has been eroded, its numbers are diminishing. In light of the past chapters, therefore, it might be worth our while to take a look at ourselves as a church, and see why we have lost so many members to the New Age movement and fundamentalist religions. Have these groups grown at our expense? Understanding a bit more about both our former glory and our present toothlessness may help us to discern the road to recovery.

The church in America has had its bad moments before, of course. In the early history of this country there were many times when the full force of anti-Catholicism was felt and people were forced to deny their faith if they wanted to eat. In the 1890s, anti-Catholic mobs in half a dozen American cities burned convents, churches, and Irish neighborhoods. Armed Irishmen, when they weren't standing guard around their parish buildings, fought pitched retaliatory battles with nativists. But we are more concerned here with the years prior to the Second Vatican Council. In a rather stunning reversal, during the decade when World War II flowed into the cold war (mid-1940s to the mid-1950s), Catholicism became the very face of postwar "Americanism." In a sudden and startling turnabout, the long-hated and long-persecuted Catholic church in America became the "in" thing. The days of glory had arrived.

This dramatic shift showed itself in the nation's most reliable indicator: popular pop culture. Take movies, for example. For three consecutive years, 1943, 1944, and 1945, movies centering on Roman Catholicism: "Song of Bernadette," "Going My Way," "The Bells of St. Mary's," and "The Keys of the Kingdom," were nominated for thirty-four Oscars and won twelve. The Catholic priest, once a sinister figure in the American imagination, actually became a cinematic model of American manhood. We see this in various characterizations: Spencer Tracy as Father Flanagan in "Boys' Town"; Bing Crosby as a crooning ex-baseball player, Father Chuck O'Malley, in "Going My Way"; Karl Malden as a labor priest in "On the Waterfront"; William Gargan as the sympathetic priest in "You Only Live Once"; and Pat O'Brien in "San Francisco," who flattens a professional fighter played by Clark Gable. From these emerged the image of the "super padre," virile, wise, good-humored, compassionate, and, in emergencies, possessed of a remarkable knockout punch. In that same period of time, you will also notice that there was not a single World War II movie where the battlefield chaplain was not a Catholic priest. The people in the foxholes were always one-third Protestant, one-third Catholic, one-third Jew; but the chaplains were always Irish Catholic priests. So what if they were celibate? So (apparently) was the Lone Ranger.

In those years, as Charles Morris points out in his marvelous book, *American Catholic*, the Catholic church was to morality and uplift what General Motors was to industry and the Yankees were to baseball. The inspiring televised lectures of Bishop Fulton J. Sheen, with a peak audience of 30 million, swamped Milton Berle's comedy hour to become the nation's most popular television program. Thomas Merton, with his 1948 book, *Seven Storey Mountain*, made conversion and monasticism popular. And of course, a few years later, there was the election of John F. Kennedy, the first Catholic president. Yes, when one spoke of "the church" nobody meant the Methodist or Episcopalian or Presbyterian church. *The* church referred to the Catholic church. It was the heyday of powerbrokers like Cardinal Spellman and Cardinal Cushing, and popularizers like Father Keller of the Christophers and Father Payton of the Rosary Crusade. Yes indeed, things Catholic were admired, even by the church's many enemies. Catholicism was riding high in those halcyon years of the 1940s, 50s, and early 60s.

What Happened?

The question, then, is this: what happened between 1945 and 1995? What happened in just fifty years to cause the Catholic church to fall from a pinnacle of power, public admiration, efficiency, and grandeur into a pit of division, impotency, and irrelevancy? What happened between the 1950s, when the best-known Catholics were convert Claire Boothe Luce and actor Pat O'Brien, and the 1990s, where today's best-known Catholics are Senator Ted Kennedy and singer/actress Madonna (and her out-of-wedlock baby, Lourdes, who was baptized Catholic)? What happened in between Bing Crosby's Father O'Malley and today's Bishop Keith Symons of Palm Beach, the first U.S. bishop to resign his diocese over charges of sex abuse? What happened between Bishop Fulton Sheen and Fr. Guido Sarducci on *Saturday Night Live*; between the the loyal faithful of the 1950s, ninety percent of whom went to Mass every Sunday, and the barely twenty-six percent of mostly gray heads who attend Mass today? (There are as many former Catholics today as there are Southern Baptists).

What happened between the overflowing rectories and seminaries and three or four priests to a parish, to the forty-eight thousand priests who left between 1964 to 1986—leaving, according to the *1998 Official Catholic Directory*, fewer than twenty-four thousand active diocesan priests, a drop of almost thirty percent from fifteen years ago? (Religious order priests have also dropped about thirty percent in fifteen years.) Today, two-thirds of American parishes have only one (aging) priest and thirteen percent of them have no resident pastor at all. What happened between the nun in every Catholic school classroom, like a chicken in every pot, to almost no nuns in *any* classroom? Today there are as many ex-nuns as nuns. What has happened in all this time? Once we were large-families, fish-on-Friday, missal-toting, novena-going, medal-wearing, fasting-from-midnight, ember-day Catholics who knew who we were. Now we have a severe identity problem, which we will explore in this chapter.

Many Theories

People have many theories about why this identity crisis occurred, ranging from the loss of the Latin Mass, to the replacement of the Baltimore Catechism with self-esteem books, to replacing the lives of the saints with secular celebrities, through the refusal to ordain women, the ban on birth control, and, of course, the all-time favorite, the Second Vatican Council. But before anyone says "Vatican II," which is putting the cart before the horse, let's take a long-range look at a more substantial and realistic reason for "what happened."

The overriding reason for the shift in Catholicism that has occurred over the last fifty years is what I call the collapse of the Total Church. That phrase, the "Total Church," is a symbol for the church many of us knew and loved, a church which had many wonderful strengths. This church lived in a culture, but was always apart from it. In fact, it had evolved its own culture within a culture. The Total Church was an all-enveloping cocoon of institutions, beliefs, and practices. Thus, we had the marvelous rhythms of the liturgical year, the habits of the nuns, the cassocks of the priests, the requirements of fasting from midnight, a strict Lent, ember days, fish on Fridays, the cult of the saints, parish missions, incense, autocratic and never-to-be-questioned pastors, precise directives from Rome, firm discipline, Catholic schools, miraculous medals, novenas, sodalities, weekly or monthly confession, the Latin Sunday Mass with its sense of mystery, the Baltimore Catechism, morning and evening prayer, the Angelus, the bowing of the head at the name of Jesus, the rosary, Marian shrines, and first Fridays. Someone described the old texture of Catholicism—at least when we met for church—this way:

> The Catholic church of yesterday had a texture to it, a feel: the smudge of ashes on your forehead on Ash Wednesday, the cool candle against your throat on St. Blaise's day, the waferlike sensation on your tongue in communion. It had a look: the oddly elegant sight of the silky vestments on the back of the priest as he went about his mysterious rites facing the sanctuary wall in the parish church; the mon-

strance with its solar radial brilliance surrounding the stark white host of the tabernacle; the indelible impression of the blue-and-white Virgin and the shocking red image of the Sacred Heart. It even had a smell, an odor: the pungent incense, the extinguished candles with their beeswax aroma floating ceilingward and filling your nostrils, the smell of olive oil, and sacramental balm. It had the taste of fish on Friday and unleavened bread and hot-cross buns. It had the sound of unearthly Gregorian chant and *flectamus genua* and mournful *Dies Irae*. The church had a way of capturing all your senses, keeping your senses and your being enthralled.

That's a picture of the Total Church (albeit the baroque church of the nineteenth century). It had a texture to it. People raised in today's churches with no definite "look" (some Catholic churches look more like Quaker meeting rooms; former White House speechwriter Peggy Noonan says they are "like Dulles airport"), with no smells (incense long gone, electric candles, deodorizers at work), sights (no earthy virgins or bleeding hearts, or any images for that matter), sounds (everyday guitars are in), and mystery ("Have a nice day" is the dismissal) can't imagine what the "texture" of the church was. But it was that way all over when Catholicism was pervasive. There existed, in short, a glorious Catholic ghetto, a vast interlocking network of what it meant to be, to act, to live and believe as a Catholic. The whole overarching, cradle-to-the-grave system was reassuring, comforting, and secure. We knew that we had the true faith, with the sacraments available at every critical step of our lives. We could spend our entire lives, from the cradle to the grave, in the cocoon of Catholic institutions, a cocoon which presented a coherent worldview and clarity about life's goal and meaning. There was certainly no Catholic identity crisis then. You knew who you were. The church was indeed "Mother" church—all caring, all embracing, all certain about what was good for you.

This is what we call the "Total Church"; this is the church older Catholics miss, the church that Catholic traditionalists are vainly trying to return to.

Internal and External Flaws

The Total Church had its strengths as well as its beauty (and, for me, sweet memories); but, alas, it also had its flaws—fatal flaws—which eventually undermined it. The flaws were twofold: internal and external. The internal flaws basically came down to certain contradictions. Let's list ten of them:

1. In the Total Church, which had started out with Jesus washing feet and saying, "the one who would rule over all must be the servant of all," there arose a very paternalistic power structure. "Catholic Action" meant participation in the mission of the bishops; it was not regarded as a right and duty of ordinary baptized disciples. "Pray, pay, and obey" was more than a clever slogan defining the relationship between authority and the people: it was a reality for Catholic laity. The church, then, was power orientated, bureaucratic, and restrictive. It had rules and rubrics which often became more important and sacred than the actual meaning of the celebrations themselves. Bishops were not to be contradicted. The distinction between the will of God and that of the priest, bishop, pope, or mother superior was blurred. The structures of the church kept adult Christians perpetually in the role of unthinking children. Many people, many priests and nuns, went to their graves with gifts untapped, unused.

2. Well, listen to this story. Abe Goldberg was in Manhattan and he not only found himself near St. Patrick's Cathedral but buffeted by a huge and jubilant crowd of thousands of

candidates for the RCIA who were about to be received into the church. Before he knew it, Abe was swept up by the momentum along the sidewalk, up the stairs and into the church. There he was propelled up the aisle with all the others, baptized, confirmed, and given holy communion. After it was all over, a bewildered Abe stumbled home. He saw his wife playing Mah-Jongg with her friends. "Sarah," he said, "you won't believe what happened to me today!" "Not now," replied Sarah, "I'm winning. Later." So he went down the hall where his son was at the computer. "Murray," he said, "you won't believe what happened to me today!" "Later, Pops," Murray said, "I'm working on my term paper." So Abe went to his daughter's room where she was dressing. "Becky," he said, "You'll never believe what happened to me today!" "Later, Dad," said Becky, "I'm late for a date." Abe went to the kitchen, stood by the sink and said to himself, "I'm a Catholic only an hour and *already* I hate these people!"

This is my way of saying that the church, founded by Jesus the Jew, was anti-Semitic (a fault which has been magnificently corrected in our time). Remember the Good Friday prayers for the "damned Jews"? The church, founded by Jesus who held fellowship meals with those "outside the law," was racist. It allowed no mixed congregations.

3. The church was (and still is) sexist. Women, who were presented as coworkers in Paul's epistles and who played important roles up to the early medieval church (one thinks of powerful abbesses like Hilda, who lived in the seventh century), were undervalued, underused, and cast in roles of inequality. They were confined to the role of either mother figure (wife, cook, housekeeper) or temptress.

4. The rights and needs of individuals were always considered secondary to the needs of the church, regardless of the psychological, emotional, spiritual, or physical well-being of the individual involved. A prime example of this could be

found in the laws concerning mixed marriages. If you married a non-Catholic, you had to be married in the rectory rather than in the church. In death, you and your spouse would have to be buried in separate graves since a non-Catholic could not be buried in consecrated ground. Many Catholics in this situation experienced a lot of a pain because of these laws, and some left the church in anger.

The institutional concerns of religion were put above spirituality, and the good name of the institutional church was placed before the rights and needs of the individual. This type of policy had the unhappy consequence of protecting unethical or immoral perpetrators, such as pedophiles. Feelings were negated, and personal rights and dignity were overlooked. Questioning was disloyal, the sign of a bad Catholic. People were valued for what they could contribute rather than for themselves. The individual came second in the Total Church.

5. Spirituality for the laity was a hand-me-down monastic spirituality, one that was essentially of the privatistic, "save my soul" kind, which was not strong on social justice. This spirituality really did not fit the everyday needs of mothers, fathers, and workers.

6. Sin, especially sexual sin and its eternal consequences, was the key aspect of that spirituality, which led to great guilt and multiple confessions. Catholic guilt—in particular, Irish Catholic guilt—became a staple for jokes. An Irish lady once said to me, "It's not a good day if you don't feel guilty." What was it that the priest said to Groucho Marx? "Thanks for giving so much joy to life." To which Groucho shot back, "Thanks for taking so much out of it."

7. The unessential became intertwined with the essential so that the two blended into one. You could go to hell for eating a hot dog on Friday, right along with a mass murderer. The St. Patrick's Day parade was on par with giving alms. Devotional practice began to resemble magic with so many

indulgences, novenas, and prayers mathematically recited to force God's hand.

8. The liturgical life of the church was skewed. Popular devotions, many of them quite lovely and moving, over-shadowed the central act of worship, the eucharist. People coming to a public building for communal worship turned the church into a private chapel as they individually recited their rosaries and prayed their novenas during Mass.

9. Ortho*doxy* was pushed at the expense of ortho*praxis*. The numerous Catholic converts to evangelical fundamentalism often say—*too often say*—"This is the first time I met Jesus Christ." Why do they shame us with that fact? Because, as Bishop Raymond Lucker said, "Too many Catholics have been catechized and sacramentalized, but never evange-lized. They have never heard the Good News of Jesus Christ…We taught them for years that you become a Catholic by learning a set of doctrines and following a set of rules. But we never taught them to know the Lord."

10. Isolation, a triumphal sense of possessing all truth, and a strident conservatism forbade any dialogue with other reli-gions—who, after all, were steeped in error. The hard-nosed centralization of Rome, with its traditional need to control and force conformity, was a fault waiting to explode in an increasingly democratic world. Only later on would the Second Vatican Council declare that the whole church "of Christ is truly present in all legitimate local congregations of the faithful." In these communities "Christ is present." Even more years later, in *Christifidelis Laicis*, would Pope John Paul II write: "The ecclesial community, while always hav-ing a universal dimension, finds its most immediate and vis-ible expression in the parish. It is here that the church is seen locally. It is necessary that in the light of faith all redis-cover the true meaning of the parish."

Still today, Roman centralization often remains oppres-sive, greatly abetted by the quality of the bishops appointed by Rome, who, by and large, are conservative in belief and practice. An interesting aside here is that the appointment of bishops by Rome is a novelty in the church. In the second century the *Apostolic Tradition of Hippolytus* flatly declared, "Let him be ordained as bishop who has been chosen by all the people." The fifth-century pope St. Celestine said, "Let a bishop not be imposed upon the people whom they do not want," and his successor as pope, St. Leo, added, "He who has to preside over all must be elected by all. Let a person not be ordained against the wishes of the Christians and whom they have not explicitly asked for." As recently as 1829, out of the six hundred and forty-six Roman Catholic bishops in the world only twenty-four were directly appointed by the pope. In reality, the pope did not receive the power to appoint all bishops until the 1917 Code of Canon Law. And even when a pope appointed a bishop before canon law was revised, he did so not as pope but as primate of Italy or as secular ruler of the papal states, because the anti-papal kings of Italy, who used to appoint the bishops, refused to do it anymore.

These, then, were some of the internal contradictions that were gradually undermining the Total Church. The wonderful strengths, the mysterious liturgy, the sacraments, the compelling "texture," all were sooner or later undermined by a church structure and unspoken assumptions that were out of sync with the times—and, truth be told, with the gospel.

The Cultural Revolution

The internal weaknesses of the Total Church were powerful conduits for deconstruction. But there were far more powerful, far more determining external forces at work, quite beyond the church's control; namely, that the whole of the American culture changed dramatically in the 1960s. Whether it was due to the Vietnam War, Watergate, the assassinations of the 60s, the explosion of the drug culture, the growth of the media, the rise of capitalism, or a confluence of all of these, there was a seismic shift in our culture from which we have not yet recovered. And although the instances cited here occurred primarily in the United States, *the coherent world, Catholic and otherwise, which existed prior to the 60s was forever changed.*

It seems to me that there are eight major reasons for this change:

1. The fall from grace of the major institutions that mediated meaning
2. The rise of corporate capitalism;
3. Modern science;
4. The breakdown of Catholic ethnic culture;
5. The homogenizing power of a global mass media and its byproduct, diversity.
6. The success of evangelical religion;
7. The loss of a sense of the sacred within the churches;
8. The "culture wars" of the post-Vatican II church.

I'd like to look at each of these in some detail.

1. *The fall from grace of the major institutions that mediated meaning.* Since the Vietnam War era, with its leading slogan, "Don't trust anyone over thirty," most major institutions have been, to this day, roundly discredited. We see how cynical we, as a nation, have become toward government and its politicians, from the lies of Vietnam to the shameless and unprecedented acts of the Clinton administration in selling government influence. (Modern day movie promo: "This is the movie the government doesn't want you to see!") This distrust of government runs from the scandals in the military

to the downfall of the FBI at Waco and on through the public admissions of greed, intimidation, and harassment of citizens by the IRS. It is also evident in the overall disgust with law, especially after the O.J. Simpson trial, as well as in education, particularly higher education which has moved from its original task of opening the mind to the utilitarian task of job preparation. And cynicism is prevalent in the demise of the institution of marriage and the family, with marriage becoming an option of many different lifestyles, subverted in a culture where divorce and abortion abound and children are a burden and a bother.

The church as an institution has been undermined, as well. Even good Catholics speak disdainfully of the "institutional church." Criticism, dissent, scandals, pedophile priests, clergy resignations, suppression of free speech, and some well-publicized bad decisions: all have added to the downfall of the institutional church as a once-powerful mediator of meaning. It is not surprising that sociological data shows dissent among Catholics to be greatest in the areas of sex and authority. In the swirling aftermath of the 1960s, all institutions—previously the bearers of stability, status quo, tradition, and meaning—have come to be seen as the enemies of freedom. The upshot is that most people today no longer find meaning in tradition or in values from the past, and they reject any form of guidance or mandates or direction that would threaten emancipation and autonomy.

2. *The rise of corporate capitalism.* Whatever benefits capitalism has brought to the world, it cannot be denied that it has done harm to the fabric of the family and community. As *Time* magazine put it:

> Capitalism not only spews out cars, TVs, and other antisocial technologies, it also sorts people into little vocational boxes and scatters the boxes far and wide. Economic opportunities is

what drew farm boys into cities and it has been fragmenting families ever since.

The breakup of families, the introduction of suburbia, and the high mobility that capitalism demands helped breed divorce and the fragmentation of the family, which is the church's basic unit. Furthermore, the success and complete dominance of worldwide corporations have smothered all the local, ethnic, religious, and biblical stories and reference points. These have been replaced by a few corporate stories and icons which shape our lives into becoming consummate consumers. One writer is accurate when he says:

> In our time, the stories that most occupy us, and may most influence us, are the stories that come to us through the media, particularly television. These are the stories of our culture, the stories that tell us who we are and what we are to value. The news programs and soap operas, the sporting events and situation comedies—*they are the default catechism for our children.* There may be some good things and some bad things on television, but in the end they are all the same in this respect: they are brought to us by people trying to sell us things. The underlying story that unites them all is the message that we are supposed to learn how to be good consumers. That, it seems, is the purpose of life. That is our duty and our joy (Martin Copenhaver, *Christian Ministry,* Sept/Oct 1997; italics mine).

3. *Modern science* has wrought vast changes in the framework by which we see and interpret reality, and this has been hard on the framework of traditional religion. The new cosmology, for example, has dethroned us as the center of the universe, something which our theology once held dear.

As we now know, we are but a speck in the cosmos of many, many universes, a tiny grain of sand on the endless dunes of the cosmic Sahara. There is no up or down, no center of the universe, simply an endless evolutionary flow.

As humans, we are *not* unique and it is arrogance to think we are the only intelligent beings in a cosmos of endless universes. Nor are we the objects of a special creation—Michaelangelo's Sistine Chapel ceiling notwithstanding. As Stephen Hawking teaches us, we are the result of the same roll-of-the-dice chance as other living things, and share the same cellular and embryonic development as birds and fishes. The new biology notices that ninety-seven percent of our genes are the same as the chimpanzee. The new medicine can replace body parts such as the heart, kidney, or lungs; designer drugs can induce the ecstasy of the saints. In Scripture, when Jesus asked rhetorically, "Who can by his own will add a cubic inch to his height?" the answer was, of course, no one. But now, modern surgery can add a cubic inch or more to one's height, just as cosmetic surgery can alter one's appearance. The new technology can produce not only flowers, vegetables, and cloned animals, but babies as well—disposing of the disappointments in the process.

The new psychology has pronounced sin obsolete—there are only early traumas, road rage, suppression, victimhood, and psychological determinates. Vice becomes virtue in another time and context: who are we to judge? Much of what was once attributed to God is now attributed to natural causes; many of the things which people once prayed for can now be done by people themselves. For some, the new global, hi-tech science appears to make religion irrelevant, and creation and life itself totally random and meaningless.

4. *The breakdown of Catholic ethnic culture.* A crushing blow was dealt to the church with the breakdown of the Catholic ethnic culture in the United States. For many years, a complex network existed among the various ethnic groups

in this country, their neighborhoods and community, and the church itself. Nationality, custom, and religion were seen as one and the same; this was the church's fundamental cohesive force. Vast pockets of Catholic Poles, Germans, Irish, Italians, and Slavic immigrants sent their kids to the parochial school, jealously preserved their national customs, attended novenas and missions decade after decade, held processions, ate ethnic foods blessed by the priest, hung crucifixes, honored patron saints, erected house shrines, and wore medals. But when the ethnic neighborhoods disappeared and people moved to the suburbs; when the grandchildren were homogenized into secular Americans who no longer spoke the language, kept the customs, went to church, and got divorced like everyone else; then the Total Church lost its glue.

5. *The homogenizing power of a global mass media and its byproduct, diversity.* In bringing about the collapse of the Total Church, we need to look at the victory of both mass media and globalization. The communications revolution and the triumph of the media have undermined the Total Church considerably. Catholics, like every other group of Americans, have been homogenized and saturated by the media. As a result, polls shows *no* difference between Catholics and the rest of the country. As George Gallup said, "You look at Catholics, and you're looking at America. Today, Catholics are as upscale as the rest of the population. Catholics reflect the views of the entire country."

A couple of years ago the *New York Times* published the result of a comprehensive research project that focused on the influence of religion on a person's ethical choices. One of their conclusions measured how American Catholics compared with other Americans in their opinions concerning such issues as the death penalty, euthanasia, nuclear weapons, welfare, education, housing, and job training. The approximately sixty million American Catholics, like most

170

mainline Protestants, came out virtually indistinguishable from the rest of Americans on all of their responses to these issues. The large-families, fish-on-Friday, missal-toting, novena-going, medal-wearing, fasting-from-midnight, ember-day Catholics of yesterday's Total Church are now indistinguishable from the general secular population in consumer habits, moral conduct, and the images that inhabit the mind. As Don Cupitt wrote in his book, *After God*:

> Writers like John Updike and Umberto Eco have suggested that in modern, media-led culture, we have in effect a return of the Middle Ages: it used to be the church that supplied everyone with an imaginary world in his or her own head; now the media do that job, with celebrity as the new sainthood (p. ix).

As a result, very few Catholics know the names of many saints or people of the Bible, much less Catholic dogma and tradition. But everyone on the globe recognizes Mickey Mouse, Coca Cola, McDonald's, Tim Allen, Princess Di, Brad Pitt, and Leonardo DiCaprio.

The American entertainment industry has a virtual monopoly on the images that influence young people throughout the world. The MTV network, for example, has an even larger audience outside the United States than it does at home. The omnipresence of the media and the secular life they so endearingly promote is so pervasive that it leaves little time for reflection, for the spirit. In a recent poll, many Catholics said that the main significance of Christmas and Easter is that they are a "time for families to get together." And how do many of your children or grandchildren spend Holy Week, the most solemn religious days of the year? Easy to answer: at Disneyland. Indeed, the "Total Church" has lost out to the culture as secular society has replaced Lourdes with Graceland, relics with Disneyland trinkets, religious habits with communal jeans, the Bible with *The Celestine Prophecy*, saints with celebrities, sacraments with crystals, confessors with *Larry King Live*, and priests with therapists. Is it any wonder that in many parts of Europe, those fabulous and grand Catholic cathedrals, churches, and shrines are now museums and restaurants?

6. The success of evangelical religion. In the past fifty years, there has been a proliferation of other religions, not to mention, as we have seen, the amorphous splash of the New Age. Of approximately sixteen hundred religions and denominations active in the United States today, about eight hundred—*half!*—were founded in our lifetime, that is, since 1965. The media have shrunk the world, introducing us to other spiritualities, traditions, and religious practices which, along with mobility and changing lifestyles, have created what we call diversity. And this refers not only to a diversity of lifestyles, beliefs, practices, and ethnic groups, but also of organized religion. Membership in most mainline Protestant churches has drastically decreased, while membership in the evangelical churches—Mormon (growing so fast they may replace Christianity in the next century), Jehovah's Witnesses, Assemblies of God, and Church of God in Christ—has jumped off the charts, claiming large numbers of former Catholics along with New Age devotees.

Fueled by the endtime millennianism, anxious to convert as many as they can before the "Rapture," evangelical fundamentalists have experienced resounding success, mostly at the expense of Catholicism. Take, for example, Latin America. In the late 1960s, there were about five million Protestants in Latin America; today there are more than forty million, and the number is growing every day. In Catholic Guatemala, thirty percent of the population is evangelical, including two recent heads of state. In Catholic Brazil, evangelicals account for around twenty percent of the population of one hundred fifty million. In Catholic Chile, between fifteen and twenty percent of the population are evangelicals. According to the evangelical Lausanne Statistical Task Force, the number of conversions to Bible-believing Christianity has risen from seventy thousand in 1991 to one hundred seventy thousand in 1994. Right now, the largest parish church in the world, seven hundred thousand strong, is the Assemblies of God church in Seoul, Korea. And due to intense evangelizing, all evidence points to the fact that by the year 2000, China will probably have the largest evangelical church in the world.

Furthermore, the American landscape is no longer predominantly Christian. There are today eight hundred thousand Hindus in this country, compared with a mere seventy thousand twenty years ago. There are as many Muslims as there are Presbyterians, and seven hundred fifty thousand Buddhists, the fastest growing Eastern religion in the United States. And in these days of enshrined relativism, who is to say which religion is right or which one is wrong? One religion seems as good as another. In another recent poll forty-eight percent of Catholics interviewed said that Catholics are essentially no different from Protestants; half said the Catholic church is no more faithful to the will of Christ than the other Christian churches.

7. *The loss of a sense of the sacred within the churches.* The collapse of the Total Church was abetted by the loss of the sacred within secular society, and sometimes even within in the church itself. We have touched on this theme before and will again. It is axiomatic in sociology that when a church marries a culture it soon becomes a widow. Or as sociologist Rodney Stark puts it in his book, *The Rise of Christianity*: "Sometimes a traditional faith and its organized expression can become so worldly that it cannot serve the universal need for religious compensators. That is, religious bodies can become so empty of supernaturalism that they cannot serve the religious needs..." (p. 39). How did this happen,

this loss of the sacred? In two ways, I think.

First, there was the slow triumph of the therapeutic over the scriptural and the mystical. For instance: in his book, *Married to the Church*, Ray Hedin writes of his clerical classmates. Noting that while a great majority of them initially chose the priesthood because it was a helping profession, this ideal "has given way for most of them to more personalist, growth-centered theologies, more akin to therapy." They came to believe that the self is not to be denied in the interest of holiness...attuned as they are to the changing culture of their own generation, most of them have come to see their own fulfillment not just as desirable but as a moral imperative" (p.118–119). These guys—priests, no less—were forerunners of the New Age!

Moral categories were replaced by therapeutic ones as the language of therapy began to replace the language of Scripture and tradition. Programs replaced spirituality. Social justice agendas replaced prayer in a kind of reversal of the tenet that if "faith without works is dead, works without faith is humanism." Secular nostrums replaced the theology of the cross. Homilies came straight out of pop psychology books. The best you could get might be a type of Christian humanism, not a radical gospel. The sacred mindset, in a word, had converted to secularism. Ronald Rolheiser humorously described this shift:

> Thus, where the contemplative (of past generations) might refer to his erotic aching as "immortal longings," the non-contemplative is more prone to speak of "being horny"; where the contemplative speaks of "a providential meeting," the non-contemplative speaks of "an accident"; where the contemplative speaks of finding "a soul mate," the non-contemplative is more prone to speak of "great chemistry"; where the contemplative speaks of "being

caught up in a painful romance," the non-contemplative is more likely to speak of "obsessional neurosis"; and where the contemplative speaks about human restlessness as a "nostalgia for the infinite and a sign of being a pilgrim on earth," the non-contemplative is more likely to feel the same discontent and wonder if he needs a career change or a new marriage (*The Shattered Lantern*, Crossroad, 1995, p. 49).

The secular and sacred cultures intermeshed so that it was not only hard to tell one from the other, but it was impossible for the sacred to witness against the culture. The mainline Protestant churches were, perhaps, the most glaring victims of the triumph of the therapeutic over the sacred, the blurring of the secular and the sacred, but Catholics were not far behind.

The second contribution to the loss of the sacred was the overarching shift in the iconic, that is, the displacement and neglect of the rich symbols of the church. This is most visibly seen in the impact of the changes in the liturgy (which, to this day, even the most dedicated proponents have admitted has suffered a loss of mystery). The shared and collaborative liturgy we now have is an incredible experience and very fulfilling for most Catholics: I would never want to see that lost. But unintended negative side effects of liturgical renewal still linger: the discarding of folkloric religion which gave outlet to human emotions; the almost complete loss of Gregorian chant; the diminishment of popular devotions; the reduction of symbolic seasons like Lent and Advent; the absences of icons in contemporary churches; the banal English translations of the Mass; and the often too extreme emphasis on the horizontal community at the expense of the transcendent.

Further, a pop-culture brand of religious education has led to one of our most serious problems in the church today:

religious illiteracy. Scott Hahn, writing of his journey from Protestant minister to Catholic convert, speaks of his Protestant proselytizing days when he took advantage of this illiteracy. He writes:

> I deliberately targeted Roman Catholics, out of compassion and concern for their errors and superstitions. When it came to leading Bible studies for the high school kids, I strategically aimed my teachings to reach Catholic young people, who I felt were lost and confused. I was especially alarmed at their ignorance—not only of the Bible but of their own church's teachings. For some reason, they didn't even know the basics of the catechism. I got the feeling that they were being treated like guinea pigs in their own CCD programs. As a result, getting them to see their church's "errors" was like shooting ducks in a barrel (*Rome Sweet Rome*, p. 14).

It is interesting to observe that the wildly successful evangelical conversions are founded on the use of basic symbols, along with an emphasis on fundamental themes of good and evil. The evangelical preachers openly wrestle with demons, preach warfare against Satan, and are not afraid to name evil spirits, a practice which is an embarrassment for most educated Catholics. The fundamentalists offer a purgative experience that is especially attractive to men. They advise abstinence from heavy drinking, sexual immorality, and financial dishonesty achieved through the once-and-for-all drama of conversion and a rigid code of morality coupled with a tight social network. This approach works because it uses basic, accessible symbols to deal with life's difficulties and tragedies, symbols which we Catholics have discarded or neglected.

For a time, few Catholics seemed to care that these symbols were lost. Yet all too obviously today, we see that many do care! In the disillusionment of the post-modern world of the Holocaust, Hiroshima, and Vietnam; in the face of the genocide in Rwanda and Bosnia and a drug, divorce, and abortion culture that is rife, people are turning to God in their search for meaning. But when they look to the churches for signs of the sacred, they too often find them copycats of the very culture they find wanting. So what do they do? Catholics turn to New Age spirituality and to TV gurus; they watch *Touched By an Angel* and make one-hundred-week best-sellers out of atrocious claptrap like *The Celestine Prophecy;* they do Eastern meditation and listen to New Age music while gazing at crystals; they consult angel calendars and the Tarot, wear "What Would Jesus Do?" bracelets, and push Christian publishing and music into a multi-billion dollar a year business. Catholics seek these options because, among other reasons, they cannot find the sacred, the mysterious, and the iconic in the church of their birth.

8. *The culture wars and dislocations of Vatican II.* It takes time to do a complete about-face from the church as institution to the church as mystery; from degrees of holiness to a universal call; from mission through ordination to mission through baptism; from top-down, unilateral directives to collaboration, solo ministry to shared ministry; from the church as hierarchy to the church as the People of God; from a universal to a local church; from "the council's gone too far" to "the council's not gone far enough." Unwittingly, the council itself unleashed principles that took the church further than the council had intended. Consider this: by making a distinction between the content of faith and its cultural expression, the council opened the door to toppling the old, rigid, scholastic expressions of faith and, in a kind of neo-Protestantism, embraced the relativity which says that faith is never really captured in any particular form for all time but is always open to subjective interpretation. There has

been, in short, a blessing of the subjective experience in the understanding of religious truth:

> For there is a growth in the understanding of the realities and the word which have been handed down. This happens through the contemplation and study made by believers who treasure these things in their hearts through the intimate understanding of spiritual things they experience. (*Constitution on Revelation*)

This was certainly a turnabout from what had been the church's steady rejection of any subjective role in grasping faith, a reversal which could (and did) lead to interpretations at variance with traditional ones. By affirming the intrinsic merit of non-Catholic religions, religious liberty, and pluralistic ideals, the council laid the foundation for indifferentism. By highlighting the primacy of conscience in moral decision-making, it was laying the groundwork for the dissent over *Humanae Vitae* and other moral issues, in effect, for the erosion of church authority.

Whether purposely or not, the council raised doubts about the merits of an expressedly religious vocation by dissolving the traditional distinctions among the degrees of holiness—the spiritual elites being the priesthood and the dedicated religious life. It democratized the "universal call to holiness," and the corporate responsibility of all Christians to redeem the world by sanctifying the secular order. Grace and nature were pronounced less and less distinct, while secular pursuits were extolled. Many priests and religious wondered: if grace and salvation were so readily "out there," what am I doing "in here"—and with such restrictions besides? By imparting legitimacy to collegiality and bowing to the culture's embrace of "personal autonomy," the council led priests and nuns, and other Catholics for that matter, to question the party line. In short, a new, more democratic church reflecting American democracy and personal autonomy, and ironically legitimized by the council itself, has replaced the Total Church.

Aggravating these dislocations within the church are what we might call "cultural wars" among Catholics themselves: Catholics for free choice, Catholics for contraception, Catholics for women's ordination, Catholics for married clergy, Catholics for gay rights—and Catholics against some or all of these things. Traditionalist Catholics, defined as critics and opponents of Vatican II, and conservative Catholics, defined as critics but not opponents of Vatican II, are pitted against liberal Catholics. Loyal Catholics are pitted against "cafeteria" Catholics. In the church today, public infighting, a declining and aging clergy, and myriad scandals have taken their toll. Here are two typical reader responses to the article "The Next Pope," which appeared in the May 11, 1998 issue of *U.S. News & World Report:*

> I grew up in Catholic school in the sixties. It was, in retrospect, a period of innocence that one enjoys just before the bottom falls out. It was the last moment when we could go out in the world protected by the certain casing of the Catholic doctrine. Today the church is a moribund institution. Its hierarchy amuses itself by creating elegant pedantic interpretations of doctrines the flock has since ceased to believe in. Pope John Paul II accomplished some things but failed at his main task, revitalizing the church and making it vital to all Catholics. If his successor continues the stagnant gerontocracy of the tradition, the church will be what it is becoming, a church in name only (written by a reader from York, Pennsylvania).

Professor Richard McBrien comments, "it will

take the church a while to recover" from insensitive Vatican domination supposedly reasserted by Pope John Paul II. This pontificate has been one of leadership, healing, reconciliation, and prophetic witness. What it will take the church a while to recover from is the centrifugal and potentially schismatic forces unleashed by what might be called the School of Modernist Triumphalism, of which Richard McBrien is a prominent spokesman (written by a reader from Tuscaloosa, Alabama).

In addition to these "culture wars," think also of the impact of the Internet. It is the very antithesis of the hierarchy that has marked the Catholic church for centuries. By that I mean that today, unilateral top-down directives are obsolete and ineffective. The fact is, people can now bypass the hierarchy altogether and, in a totally democratic manner, can instantly and directly connect with one another on the global Internet and voice whatever opinions or disagreements they wish. In a wired world, unconsulted, uninformed, one-way solo pronouncements are irrelevant, as are attempts to control thoughts or screen out alternatives. The Internet, in a word, has flattened out the force of the central authority of the church.

Fallout from the Cultural Revolution

What all these internal and external reasons for the collapse of the Total Church amount to is this: since the sixties, there has been a cultural revolution and the Catholic Church—in fact, all churches—has been the victim of that. The revolution started when things got out of control—Vietnam, assassinations, race relations, the questioning of institutions—and theologians began to declare that God was dead. At the same time people were being exposed to new ideas and information on an unprecedented scale. Spirituality, which was formerly highly territorial (shrines, retreat houses, parish churches, synagogues, mosques) and connected to the stable neighborhood and, as we have seen, the ethnic ghetto, gave way to the fluidity of contemporary life. A "sacred place" became wherever and whatever "centered" a person.

As a result of this cultural revolution, there is a smorgasbord of lifestyles and spiritualities competing for the attention of Catholics, each of which is wildly ecumenical. The diversity of lifestyles and spiritualities is especially attractive to those who found their stable, ghetto-ized, self-contained systems too narrow, too controlling, too exclusive, and indeed, too intolerant (of women, homosexuals, blacks, the divorced). Many young people are eager to jettison the ethnic, religious, and racial prejudices of their churchgoing parents. They have become aware that spirituality and organized religion are different and perhaps even hostile to one another. They tend to see spirituality as broad-based, drawing insights from many sources, whereas religion may seem but a particular institutional manifestation of different traditions. In short, religion has become identified with denominationalism, while spirituality represents the common core of humanity.

One thing that most of us know for sure is that organized religion does not give answers to the new problems of society, for example, the environment; maybe answers lie elsewhere, say, with the Native Americans or Zen Buddhists or the like. That is why many people, especially those who are still young, claim their spirituality is growing while the impact of religion on their lives is diminishing.

So, forsaking their inherited religion, the post-sixties generations piece together their faith like a patchwork quilt as each seeks his or her own spiritual way. Having learned that they can move around and think through their options, they adopt a rather freewheeling and eclectic style of spirituality as they try out various religions and taste the offerings of the latest guru. Choice is emphasized and promoted in everything: abortion, lifestyles, living arrangements, jobs, sex, dress, and, above all, consumerism. Why not? It was in the 1960s, after all, after the scarcities of the Second World War, that retailing on a massive scale took place. The generation of the 60s was the first to come of age during a fully advertised consumer society. They have been exposed to television since birth and prosperity has given them the opportunity to explore every offering. "Freedom of choice" has become the mantra of the liberated world, taking our young people outside the traditional social institutions which used to mediate meaning. They have been nourished on the primacy of individual "rights" ever since the civil rights movement. They have become seekers in a culture where denominational differences and doctrines are becoming less and less important than, say, serving others. As Robert Wuthnow describes it:

> There are many ways of experiencing the shift from dwelling to seeking. For some people, the shift is experienced as living no longer within sacred space but between sacred spaces. At one time, people were residents of their communities; now they are commuters. Thus images of stable dwellings have increasingly been replaced by images of those who have left home: the migrant worker, the exile, the refugee, the drifter, the person who feels alienated or displaced, the person lost in the cosmos, the traveling salesman, the lonesome net surfer, the lonely face in the crowd, the marginal person, the vagrant, the dispossessed or homeless person.

> The same is true of spirituality. At one time,

people identified their faith by membership; now they do so increasingly by the search for connections with various organizations, groups, and disciplines, all the while feeling marginal to any particular group or place. For some people, the shift is analogous to changes that have taken place in the economy. They no longer depend primarily on producing durable goods; instead, they produce services and information. In their faith, they once relied heavily on bricks and mortar, on altars, and on gods who were likened to physical beings and who called them to dwell eternally in sacred places. Now they concentrate on information flows—ideas that help with the particular needs they have at the moment but that do not require permanent investments of resources.

Other people experience change as a shift from spiritual production to spiritual consumption. They used to produce offspring for their churches and synagogues, send out missionaries and evangelists to convert others, and spend their time working for religious committees and guilds; they now let professional experts—writers, artists, therapists, spiritual guides—be the producers while they consume what they need in order to enrich themselves spiritually.

In other ways, the shift from dwelling to seeking influences images of what it means to be spiritual. Faith is no longer something people inherit but something for which they strive. It provides security not by protecting them with high walls but by giving them resources, by

> plugging them into the right networks, and by
> instilling the confidences to bargain for what
> they need. (*After Heaven*, University of
> California Press, 1998, pp. 7-8)

For many people today, spirituality is a negotiated spirituality. They are convinced that organized religion cannot solve their problems, so they must figure out their own lives. Still, through all this eclecticism, one point remains: spirituality is riding high. Life is enormously complex—two-career couples and single parents juggle family responsibilities, not knowing what is right or wrong; and evil looms everywhere—drugs, crime, children killing children, and moral indifferentism. Lacking a community or set of teachings they consider authoritative, people seek signs: miracles which are reassuring and make them feel good (no awe or fear here), angels who are basically buddies but who nevertheless remind them that a higher, more meaningful reality exists over and above their everyday, technical lives. We remain fascinated with manifestations of the sacred because, when you come right down to it, we are uncertain about whether the sacred is still around.

There we have it. *That's* what happened between Father O'Malley and Father Guido, between the flawed but coherent 1940s to the splintered and unfocused 1990s. The Total Church could only survive when there was a consensus of what was right and wrong, where there were common values and shared goals. It could only survive in an ethnic ghetto and with static isolation, in the village where it was the majority, where it had the "true religion" and everyone else was in error. Once that ghetto broke up, once other lands were discovered, other religions studied, and other virtues recognized in other places and peoples, the Total Church was on its way out. Once people realized that, in a world context, Christianity was but a minority religion *and had no monopoly on spirituality*, and that each particular denomination is a minority within that minority; once the newly invented mass media opened other realities and possibilities for personal growth, human potential, and alternate religious experience; above all, once the global marketplace broke down the ethnic patterns and the ghetto walls, leaving religion and secular society indistinguishable from one another, then the days of the Total Church were numbered. Catholic identity was up for grabs.

And lo and behold, here we are, caught in the confused throes of the demise of the Total Church.

The New Catholic Identity

With so much homogenization and so much loss of the specifics that used to point us out as different, Catholic identity is indeed a serious concern. Leading sociologists and Catholic laypersons met in England in the summer of 1998 to discuss why membership in the Catholic church in England has plummeted since the 1950s, like ours in the United States. This gathering raised the same issue of Catholic identity. Why, they asked, have so many left the church? What has drawn people away? A report gives this account:

> Speakers at the conference, organized by the sociologist Michael Hornsby-Smith, gave papers on the changes that have occurred in patterns of family and parish life, schools and lay organizations in the demography of the church and its national role. Two of the main themes to emerge were a loss of Catholic identity and a frustration, which occurred after Vatican II, with the authority of the church.
>
> The loss of a specifically Catholic identity was charted by Frank Boyce, the former dean of

Hopewood Hall...He described how in the 1930s, devotions such as Benediction, the Forty Hours and the Stations of the Cross were a source of sensory pleasure for local people. He quoted an interviewee who recalled that era: "The parish churches were like people's palaces. In another way, it was like going to the big picture houses in town with their deep carpets and chandeliers and the usherettes in their nice dresses. Going to church and going to the pictures took you out of yourself." (*The Tablet*, 13 June, 1998, p. 793)

In one way the quest for a religious identity is as old as humankind itself, and is marked by an ongoing struggle between accommodation and withdrawal. The religious history of the Jews, for example, is full of conflicting questions: Shall we accommodate ourselves to the Babylonians, Greeks, or Romans? Or shall we form our own enclaves? Will we be absorbed and lose our identity? Or will we be separatist and save it? How should a Jew act? What made one righteous? On all these issues, people took sides.

Christians fare no better. Since the time of Jesus similar questions have raged: what does it mean to be a Christian? How should one act? How much should Christians adopt the culture and evangelize it? Or will they in turn be evangelized by the culture? When Christianity was an underground religion fighting for its life, there was no identity crisis. But once the Roman imperial government approved it and adopted it, the scenario changed. Some, like the first Christian historian, Eusebius, in the fourth century, followed the evangelist Luke in opting for accommodation, suggesting that the Roman empire was indeed "foreordained" to be a vehicle of the faith. Both Eusebius and Luke saw the Roman empire as an instrument of God's providence (the first American settlers would say the same of the new land); one indeed could be both a full citizen and a Christian. Others were not so sure. Following the author of the book of Revelation, who saw the Roman empire as a beast and a harlot, they saw danger and opted for distrust. These people fled to the desert and founded separatist monasteries. There were big names on both sides of the argument. The well-known theologian Origen was for accommodation; St. Augustine decidedly was not. (The *City of God* could brook no accommodation with the temporal city.)

Our dilemma today is similar, but played out in a global, market-run media which provides us with metaphors, stories, and values for life. Do we accommodate them or resist or find some middle ground? Truth be told, it is as difficult to resist the culture as it is for fish to resist water. It is just there, in living color, a full sophisticated context that defines who we are. Some people, of course, do resist. Some along the way choose the contemplative life, others choose separatist communities, and others join close-knit religious congregations with strong leadership, control, and the cornerstone of the Bible to hold it all together. In contrast, some simply surrender and luxuriate in an MTV-Playboy-consumerist philosophy. Yet most people muddle somewhat uncomfortably between the two poles, materialists with an uneasy hunger for God.

Every self-aware group worries about absorption; every group, sooner or later, succumbs to the culture. Perhaps Catholics can find a parallel to their loss of identity in the plight of today's Jews. In the United States today, Jews make up two percent of the population, down from four percent sixty years ago. Their supporting structures have collapsed as Jewish neighborhoods yielded to suburbanization. Social and economic mobility has widened the pool of prospective gentile spouses (fifty-three to fifty-eight percent of all Jews marry outside the faith), and rabbinical training has by and large been replaced with secular higher education. After-school religious training, like the Catholic CCD classes, is now mainly remembered "as the place where Hebrew wasn't learned" (Leonard Fein). A recent book by Alan M. Dershowitz is aptly titled, *The Vanishing American Jew: In Search of Jewish Identity for the Next Century.* You could easily change the words "Jew" and "Jewish" to "Catholic" here.

What Do Young Catholics Believe?

Another facet of shaping a new Catholic identity that must be taken seriously is the formal and informal religious education of our young people. We are paying for decades and decades of neglect in Catholic intellectual and spiritual formation, another effect of the collapse of the Total Church. Here is a case in point: a nationwide poll of young Catholics published in the July 17, 1998 issue of *Commonweal,* reveals little commitment to the church establishment. Only forty-eight percent of the young respondents identified "the necessity of having a pope" as basic to the faith, and only forty-two percent said it was essential to believe that "Christ established the authority of the bishops by choosing Peter." "What is interesting here," said William Dinges, one of the professors in charge of the poll, "is that it does point to a kind of lessened institutional sense of being Catholic." Translation: once more, Catholic identity is weakened. To disagree with or dislike a particular pope is a far cry from dismissing that office altogether since the papacy is surely one of the basic foundational elements of Catholicism. It's like dismissing the very notion of the office of president as irrelevant and nonessential to the democratic system. This blase attitude surely reflects a distrust of institutions, which we have previously noted, as well as a heady individualism.

Dinges further notes: "There is a sizable part of the young adult Catholic population that has a very denominational sense of Catholic identity...they see Catholicism as by and large another form of religious preference, and it isn't necessarily more true or more valid than any other kind of denominational religious preference...They also tend to mimic the larger cultural trend, and that is the tendency on the part of many people to simply reduce religion to ethics, to being a good person. Again, the argument being that it really doesn't matter whether you're a Methodist or Catholic or Episcopalian. What matters is—are you a good person?"

In their survey, by the way, Dean Hoge, William Dinges, and their associates also came up with a list (in descending order of importance from one to nineteen), of the way young Catholics (those between the ages of twenty and thirty-nine) rank the tenets and teachings of Catholicism. Here are some rankings: first on the list are the sacraments, seen as *the* sign of Catholic identity. Second, rating right up there with the sacraments, are service and works of charity. Third is Christ present in the eucharist, and fourth is Mary. Seventh is the necessity of the pope, and twelfth is the importance of the saints. Way down on the list, fourteen, is confession to a priest. Now, in view of what the church teaches as important, here is where things get interesting: fifteenth in importance are the reasons why abortion is wrong; sixteenth is the need for a celibate priesthood; seventeenth are the reasons for being against the death penalty; and eighteenth is the need for only male priests. There certainly seems to be a wide disparity between what the church teaches as most important and the beliefs of young Catholic adults!

What is quite obvious in this survey, refreshingly, is that among young Catholic adults the faith is still wonderously strong, as are religious needs and high ideals. There really aren't that many young adults leaving the Catholic faith—those who do mainly do so because they marry someone from another denomination. Most of the young people surveyed just plain like being Catholic, even if they disagree with the importance of the church's official teachings. The biggest complaint of these young adults is that they have little association with their parishes; although parishes have a lot of programs for children, married couples, and older adults, there is usually little offered for young adults. (Parishes take note.)

What can the parish do to help young people—as well as adults—restore their Catholic identity? Several ways seem obvious: the development of a stronger devotional life; opportunities for spiritual direction; the formation of small faith-sharing communities; an introduction to our mystical tradition; the encouragement (and example) of abstinence from meat on Fridays; a reintroduction of eucharistic devotions; and strong visual imagery (icons and symbols) in the church. In the words of Frank Boyce (see p. 186), the church needs to reclaim itself as "a source of sensory pleasure for local people." It is far better that the parish encourages and inaugurates these types of initiatives than leave them to the fringe groups, with their sentimental and compulsive mandates that pass for Catholic piety.

Another area which the church should pay attention to is music; as we well know, it is the lingua franca of the young all around the globe. We need to encourage good composers to come up with powerful music that both rallies and binds our Catholic congregations. Along those same lines, we also need to promote and use what is good in the culture, which can offer us many things and open up exciting vistas. Of course, the culture, like the church itself, must always be under the judgment of God's Word. Finally—and here we go back to the second most important thing to young people, according to the survey cited above—we must be visible agents of charity. We must continue to assist victims of the culture: those wounded by drugs, greed, promiscuous sex, easy divorce, or glorified violence. This charity, you recall, is what caught the attention of the pagans: "See how those Christians love one another."

Where Do We Go From Here?

Rodney Stark has shown that Christianity was successful because of the appeal of its compassion. In his Civil War diary, Abraham Lincoln speaks the same thought for our times:

> Of all the forms of charity and benevolence seen in the crowded wards in the hospitals, those of some Catholic Sisters were the most efficient...More lovely than anything I have seen in art...are the pictures of those modest sisters going on their errands of mercy among the suffering and dying. They were veritable angels of mercy.

To do all these things with a sense of tradition behind us, fortified through retreats, prayer, and a strong communal parish life might help the restoration process—not to mention the courage Catholics need to take a prophetic stance. We have noted previously in this book how the conservative churches freely take a countercultural position and are willing to pay the price for it. They stand in contrast to the culture-friendly progressive churches, who simply mirror the dominant culture and are reluctant to hold it up to judgment. As the editor of *Priests & People* magazine (July, 1998) chides us:

> It might be more honest to admit that the churches themselves have been deeply influenced by our national idolatries. We need to keep in mind the note which the Princess [Diana] had placed on her desk, "You can't comfort the afflicted without afflicting the comfortable." It can be disturbing to preach a Jesus who challenged his own people in their synagogue at the beginning of his ministry. He wanted

them to recognize God working, not just among themselves but also among the foreigners they would prefer to exclude, the Sidonian widow and Naaman the Syrian leper (Luke 4).

But such prophetic ministry is risky. It is safer to make religion serve our commercial instincts; here there are plenty of biblical precedents. At Ephesus, when the silversmiths' trade which depended on the cult of the local goddess, was threatened by Paul's preaching of the gospel, the local crowd went berserk. A single cry came from them all. For up to two hours they kept shouting, "Great is Diana…" (Acts 19:34). The prophet challenged the way religion was being used for idolatrous ends, so Paul, like Jesus, has to get out of town.

If the church is going to satisfy our deepest needs it must listen to the prophetic voices who bring us into contact with the disturbing presence of the God of judgment and compassion who shapes us according to his desire not ours. Then our worship must mediate that divine presence not just by words but through ritual which uses the rich and powerful symbols of the liturgy to articulate our joy and grief and pain. And finally we need a faith in the risen and crucified Christ which will connect our lives not just with the transient stories of the daily soap operas but with a much older tradition and with a much wider vision which offers the hope of an eternal life beyond death and which transcends the frenzy of the latest media event.

Speaking of identity, George Bush tells the story of how

one day, when he was president, he was doing his public relations thing by visiting a nursing home. There he came upon a wizened old man hobbling down the corridor. President Bush went up to the man, took his hands in his own, looked soulfully into his eyes and said, "Sir, do you know who I am?" The man replied, "No, but if you ask one of the nurses, she'll tell you." (At this point we needed a bit of humor.)

Making Our Way

Back to our dogs on the porch from the beginning of this chapter. Are we as a church destined to be forever toothless and impotent as the cats come and go? Movements and "isms," defections and losses: are these to be our lot? For a response let us once more turn to author Charles Morris, whom we have quoted before. He writes:

> The story of American Catholicism is therefore a story of the rise and triumph of a culture and of the religious crisis that has ensued in the wake of that culture's breakdown. Most of the church's well publicized recent problems—the financial, sexual, and other scandals that are blazoned across the front pages—can be understood as the floundering of an institution suddenly *forced to make its way solely* as a religion, shorn of the cultural supporters that had been the source of its strength.

That's the critical phrase: "to make its way solely as a religion." If we have learned anything at all from what I have written, we know in our hearts that the alliances between altar and throne are gone. Also gone are the cultural supports and power plays, the privileges and titles and affectations. We're on our own now. And the hopeful message is: who's to say that this is a bad thing? Who's to say that it's not altogether fortuitous to find ourselves, on the brink of the twenty-first century, very much like the Christians of the *first* century: starting from scratch, building from the bottom up, on the ashes of what has been, and cultivating the green sprouts of the next millennium?

The powerful use force, and we have been there. The powerless must use persuasion; we've been there too, most notably in the first centuries of the church. We as church must now be a *persuasive* people, in the spirituality of our lives, the witness of our communities, the compassion of our outreach, and the way that we live as part of a church. The great Christian minister, Jim Wallis, has it right when he writes:

> When I was a university student, I was unsuccessfully evangelized by almost every Christian group on campus. My basic response to their preaching was, "How can I believe when I look at the way the church lives?" They answered, "Don't look at the church; look at Jesus." I now believe that statement is one of the saddest in the history of the church. It puts Jesus on a pedestal apart from the people who bear his name. Belief in him becomes an abstraction removed from any demonstration of its meaning in the world. Such thinking is a denial of what is most basic to the gospel: the incarnation. People should be able to look at the way we live and begin to understand what the gospel is all about. Our lives must tell them who Jesus is and what he cares about.

The traditionalists, who *do* offer trenchant critiques and who do have a lot of wise things to say to us, are wasting their time yearning for the "good old days" (by which they really mean the baroque, cocooned church of the 1940s and 50s).

No, history helps us understand the paths to truth and engages us with a rich past and perspective. History helps come to terms with the fact that we, the church of today, are exactly like the early church; we are now a persecuted minority, a giant without weapons, an organization without influence, a people without power. And ultimately, we will overcome the obstacles before us because people will look at us and gasp, "See how those Christians love one another." That is our strength for the future.

Indeed, there *are* many powerful and significant signs that a new church is rising phoenix-like from the ashes of the old church. For one thing, there are the beginnings of a great revival of our mystical tradition along with the development of an everyday spirituality to meet the very palatable hunger for God so evident today. There is widespread interest in retreats, third orders, spiritual direction, and Bible study. There is a vast lay ministry movement and a proliferation of small faith-sharing communities. Democratic synods, pastoral councils, and parish councils are at work in the church. There is a renewal of parish life founded on a network of shared and collaborative ministry. Remember, too, there are still some thirty million Catholics who attend Mass regularly and therefore constitute the single largest denomination in the United States. Or, as Michael Novak points out: "For comparison's sake, take the ten biggest audiences in the history of television—for one of the Super Bowls, for instance: none has ever matched the number of Americans attending church and synagogue on any given weekend." Again, the words of Charles Morris:

> American Catholicism is the only successful form of Catholicism in the world. ...In Europe and Latin American, people don't identify themselves with the church. In this country, where's it's a chosen religion, it really seems to work...The church in America is still a suc-

cess—even with the priest shortage. Church attendance here is as high as anywhere. The core Catholics are probably the "best ever." They're your Vatican II *Gaudium et spes* model....

So the Catholic church in America is weak, but we are strong in numbers. We are invisible, but we are everywhere. We no longer belong to a church, but we are church, all of us, lay and cleric. We don't belong to the pastor's parish: he belongs to ours. We don't share in the bishops' mission: we are the missionaries. We no longer just receive from the top: the top is also nourished by us. We are not a pyramid: we are a circle. We are not just parishioners, but by virtue of our baptism, collaborative ministers. We have indeed been brought low. But, truth to tell, *there*, and nowhere else, will we find the feet to be washed.

8

"Partial Church" Struggles

Two men looked out of their prison bars.
The one saw mud, the other stars.
—Percy Bysshe Shelley

A young rabbi was completely dismayed to find serious division and quarrels among his new congregation. You see, during the Friday evening services half of the participants would stand during one part of the proceeding and the other half would be seated, and all semblance of decency and decorum was lost as they shouted at each other to conform to their way. Members of each group insisted that theirs was the correct tradition. Seeking guidance, the young rabbi took a representative from each side to visit the synagogue's founder, a ninety-year-old rabbi living in a nursing home. "Rabbi, isn't it true that tradition was always with the people who stand at this point of the service," asked the man from the standing-up side. "No, that was not the tradition," the old man replied. "Then it is true for people to stay seated," rejoiced the sitting-down representative. "No," the rabbi said, "that was not the tradition." "But, rabbi," cried the young rabbi, "what we have now is complete chaos. Half the people stand and shout while the other half sits and screams." "Aha!" exclaimed the old man, "*that* was the tradition!"

If we no longer have a Total Church, we might assume that what we are left with is a Partial Church. Issues such as the New Age, the success of evangelical fundamentalism, apocalyptic scenarios at variance with the church, the collapse of the Total Church and its factious aftermath, the anguish of traditionalist Catholics and the perplexity of many mainline ones, and a thoroughgoing secularization leave the church half shouting and half screaming as it pursues these questions: where does it all leave us, and where does it all lead us? One answer is that these issues leave us pondering tradition, but they also lead the church to the strategies it must tap to reclaim itself anew. And that will be the theme of this chapter as I take off the professor's hat and don the pastor's hat. With a very focused eye on the basic unit of the church, the local parish, and following the thoughts of Tom Sweetser, let me hazard some personal, practical suggestions—sixteen in all!—for renewing the church from the inside out.

1. *Reflect on the modern, post-Christian context.* Take a good objective look around you. Paradoxically, as we have noted, there is a decline in organized religion while at the same time, a deep interest in spirituality. Again, look at the phenomenal success of the New Age. Although there is deep hunger for the transcendent, people are looking to "alternate" religions outside the mainstream. As we have seen in earlier chapters, mainstream Christian religions are in decline. Protestantism has suffered major losses; there are more ex-Catholics than Southern Baptists, and more ex-nuns than current ones; the second largest denomination in the United States is non-practicing Catholics. Among rank and file Catholics in the United States, almost three-fourths of them do not celebrate Sunday liturgy with us. Statistically, we Catholics are no longer a eucharistic people.

For example, let's look at Ireland, the most Catholic country in the world. Convents and other church buildings there are regularly listed for sale, a seminary has closed, and the famed Maynooth College has the lowest intake of students in its two-hundred year history. Only sixty percent of the Irish go to church regularly—which doesn't sound so bad until you make comparisons with Ireland's recent past. The sixty percent attendance is compared to seventy-seven percent only four years ago, eighty-seven percent fifteen years ago, and ninety-one percent twenty-five years ago. Among fourteen- to eighteen-year-olds, only thirty-seven percent attend Mass weekly, and among twenty-five- to thirty-eight-year-olds the figure is thirty-eight percent.

This decline in church attendance holds true for another famously Catholic country, Canada, or at least Catholic Quebec. This clip comes from a recent newspaper article:

> At one time, Catholicism was so confident in Quebec that many envisioned it crusading to convert Protestant America. But today the pews are almost empty, the church is largely ignored, and some churches and chapels have already been converted into museums. It happened fast—within a decade—and church leaders are only now beginning to pick up the pieces...

Further on in the article, a twenty-one-year-old Quebec woman echoes the feelings of many other young people: "I believe in God, but not in the church." She says her grandparents go to Mass every Sunday, her parents rarely go, and she never does. In this behavior she is following Quebec's parent country, France, "the eldest daughter of the church," where the Catholic church and monasticism once flourished. But France has long since disengaged itself from the church. Today only a miniscule fourteen percent of the population attend Mass regularly, nearly half of all couples live together before marriage (many never marrying at all), and abortion is legal. In the U.S. the percentage of young Hispanics who describe themselves as Catholics has dropped from seventy-eight percent in the early 1970s to sixty-seven percent today. Throughout the Western world, once a stronghold of Catholicism, Mass attendance has declined. This reflects the trend noted in a recent study from Duke University Divinity School, which found that young adults in the United States hold that people who have God in their lives don't need the church.

The parish is no longer center stage, but now a vast marketplace of ideas and distractions. Everybody in parish life knows how hard it is to get people out these days even for "required" first communion or confirmation parent meetings. You're fighting single parent homes, both parents working, commuting schedules, and the twin addictive fascinators, TV and the computer. (This reminds me of the father who complained to his neighbor: "Things were a lot different when I was a boy. My son has a color TV, a home movie set, a stereo, several radios, a computer, and a telephone in his room. When I want to punish him, I have to send him to my room!") You're fighting family disruption and/or indifference to religion, a condition which lays the groundwork for either church affiliation or a lack of it. In the Duke University study mentioned above, it was shown—to no one's surprise—that one's perception of religion may indeed lie in what may have been his or her experience of family. For instance, "family disruption" was experienced by twenty-three percent of those born before 1946, twenty-seven percent of those born between 1946 and 1963, and forty-five percent of those born between 1964 and 1979. Could disruptive family life be negatively influencing the churchgoing patterns of today's Catholics?

The church exists in a swirl of competing ideologies. The parish is but one voice in the midst of temples, mosques, Home Depot, Price Club, Disneyland, chat rooms, McDonald's, designer clothing stores, and MTV. Remember the poll I cited back in chapter seven, which showed that many Catholics feel the main significance of Christmas and

Easter is that they are a "time for families to get together." This same poll also showed that only thirty percent of our young people knew what Easter was about. They responded that Easter did not celebrate the resurrection of Jesus Christ; rather, it celebrates spring, school spring break, the Easter Bunny, and so on.

It is obvious that we need to face facts and stop operating as if the parish were the medieval parish of the 1500s or the neighborhood parish of the 1950s with a full rectory, a full school, a formidable CYO, and persuasive moral authority. This is simply not so anymore. The parish today is, by and large, characterized by mostly gray heads, a struggling school (if it's still open), and a depleted, aging clergy who, like Rodney Dangerfield, "get no respect." Catholicism is a minority religion in a secular world whose splendid, technically sophisticated images, icons, and corporate storylines dominate our lives. Now, let's not get depressed about all this; the truth is, a reality check is a good place to start. We have to accept the fact that the Catholic church is in one of those major transitional periods of history and we are displaying the usual signs of dislocation, grief, and confusion. It is, for both church and society, a crisis time, a time of both danger and opportunity.

2. *Change your identity, the way you see yourself.* We are no longer power brokers. We are, in fact, as we pointed out before, very much like the Christians of the first century. Once more, we are a minority without power, prestige, political, or cultural support in a very, very pluralistic society, operating no longer from power but from weakness. From the first Christians, then, we must rediscover the ways in which they overcame obstacles.

3. *As Tom Sweetser puts it, we must change our attitude from "in here" to "out there."* Here we might ask, how would Jesus handle the problem? The answer is, Jesus moved out to the fringe—to the unwashed, the marginalized, those out-

side the law. In a sense, the parish must do the same. There must be a shift from an "in here," in-house mentality to an "out there," reaching-out approach; from a need to bring the people to the parish as much as a need to bring the parish to the people. Put the person who is immersed in family, work, travel, sports, and the Internet on center stage. The parish should be related to that world. Further, too many parishes view their task as bringing the faith to the people rather than helping people discover how faith is a natural part of what it means to be human. People *already* have faith; they need help in making sense of it. All this means that there must be a change of mindset for the pastor and staff as they struggle with the question: how do we get the parish to the people? How do we change their cultural assumptions?

As the parish staff sits down at the beginning of each new church year and considers the needs of the people, they must remember that these people generally have a deep hunger for God. This may mean letting go of some cherished projects and programs that are perhaps too in-house. The pastor and staff should put themselves in other people's shoes, find out what their needs are, and appreciate their lifestyles and opinions, even if they don't always agree with them.

The staff may also need to bring in random people and ask their help in planning for the parish. We can no longer rely totally on the staff to make parish plans—not because its members aren't capable, but because the pastor and staff are often too close to the parish, too much the "insiders" to be objective. One way to invite others in is to send out fifty or so letters to random people, actively involved in the parish or not, asking them to come and just talk about the parish. Once the group is gathered, brainstorm about the parish, its needs and its future, ideas and strategies. Then bring the results to the staff for further comment and refinement. This procedure brings the parish leadership beyond its in-house vision and concerns. The church is wise to get out of the management business, trying to run everything itself. It must now join collaboratively with others in faith and in charity.

4. *Remember the old truism for conversion: affiliation, not argument, is the way to go.* All sociological data prove what common sense has always known: people are not converted by dogma (that comes later) but by affiliation with believing family members, friends, or an obviously caring community. If you want a practical example, think of the RCIA candidates in your parish. There is always a preponderance of fiancees and spouses, right? Just as people are attracted though human connections, so are they attracted to friendly, personable congregations and warm ministries. In a practical sense, this means creating a family atmosphere in the parish, particularly in its hospitality to long-term members and strangers alike, its church symbols, and its sacramental times. It means establishing a new ritual that welcomes back people who have started to go back to church again. It means nurturing small faith-sharing groups.

Creating a family atmosphere also means smaller parishes. I have seen many parishes throughout the United States where there are anywhere from three to eight thousand families on the rolls. These parishes are often presided over by one aging pastor and one associate pastor. Even with the fullest of lay ministries, large parishes are intrinsically the enemies of community, and the leakage, as we have noted, is great. One of the attractions of the small fundamentalist churches is the sense of community they have, where people feel known, cared about, and cared for. To recover our ground as a viable, caring church, we need not only small faith-sharing communities but smaller parishes where the eucharist can be celebrated intimately and the priest or eucharistic minister can address most people by name when giving communion. This, in turn, must put the focus on the necessity for more people who can preside at the eucharist; which, in turn, means ordaining married men, proven men who are put forth as candidates by the community. Every day that the wonderful charism of celibacy, one which only a few can accept ("Let anyone accept this who can" Matthew 19:12), dominates over the people's right to the eucharist is one more day that we become less and less a eucharistic community.

5. *A sense of the Christian sacred has to be born afresh.* We need to revisit the threshold of the Spirit. Guided by the Spirit we must become a people who keep faith with the liturgical reforms and restore the devotional life of the parish, resulting in a new respect for the sensuous and the sacramental—from the giving of ashes to the blessing of the animals. Why must we do this? First, because the Mass itself is simply not enough, and second, because the revised liturgy has been less than successful. We need to acknowledge this truth, not only with traditional Catholics but also with many liberal ones as well. As Robert Burns writes in *U.S. Catholic* (July, 1998): "Some Catholics, clerical and lay, while continuing to thank God for the window-opening of the Second Vatican Council, sometimes wonder if, in the liturgy, we may have thrown out both the baby and the bathwater." Then, quoting Bishop Kenneth Untener of Saginaw, Michigan, Burns writes, "The turning around of the altar 'in your face' and the translation of the Mass into the vernacular 'literally intruded on prayer.' With Vatican II 'the idea was, "We'll do it all together now," but we don't. We said, "This will be great." Well, it hasn't been. Twelve people in our liturgies have more actions. The other thousand have less to do.'" Burns further quotes a teacher from Ireland named Joe Coy whose children find the Mass boring—as do many adults. He says:

Church services at present can be very sterile.

The appeal is to the rationale and literacy—there is little room for feelings or emotions, nothing to lift us beyond ourselves—not enough color, light, music, sound, or scent, not enough atmosphere. Why can't the atmosphere generated by the solemn novenas, for example, be achieved on a regular basis?

Michael Paul Gallagher expresses the same thought more academically:

> Looking back now at some of the "renewal" of religious life or of liturgy that took place in the decade after the Second Vatican Council, it can be asked whether it did not embrace a certain secularization too rapidly. In those overdue and necessary efforts at pastoral relevance, one could hold that valuable aspects of tradition were unwisely discarded. Even to raise this issue can seem "restorationist," as if wanting to put the clock back. But it need not be so.
>
> In the urgency to emerge from the excessively closed culture of pre-conciliar Catholicism, a certain "acculturation" seems to have taken place: the influence of the secular liberalism of the sixties caused such an unbalanced emphasis on individual expression that genuine elements of Christian anthropology were abandoned. It is not just a superficial question of religious dress or of folk music in the liturgy: these are transitory and secondary issues. More serious was an undervaluing of symbolic languages for the sacred or an insensitivity to the need for some counter-cultural structures if spirituality is to survive. Ultimately at stake was the inescapable

differentness of the gospel way: it transcends common sense, challenges all merely human values to conversion, and creates an inevitable tension with the assumptions of a non-religious culture. In this light some of the undiscerning assimilation of the anti-structural, anti-symbolic, and anti-spiritual culture of the sixties now seems to be an example of "innocent acceptance."

His words hearken back to our last chapter where we lamented the loss of the sense of the sacred in the Catholic church, the loss of its "texture." Now we can add that this loss is best advertised in a boring, nondescript liturgy which, adopting the current cultural "in your face" democracy, subverts both the sensuous and the transcendent. Maybe that is why this generation of Catholics is fascinated with the religious lore and rituals of its grandparents, with litanies, benediction, the mystics, and the lives of the saints. Look at how the death of Princess Diana revealed society's need for ritual, even as her cult quickly descended into paganism and a subsequent industry of memorabilia. (As an aside, one could not help but notice that at her moving funeral the secular dominated and quite overwhelmed the beautiful Church of England funeral liturgy. There were personal readings by her sisters, the pop song "Candle in the Wind" sung by Elton John, the Welsh song "Cwm Rhondda," a political, hard-edged talk by her brother, and endless references to the Princess. But even in the Dean of Westminster's long commendation, there were precious little references to God. Glaringly missing from the whole service was any specifically Christian message.)

Ritual provides structure and creates community, and so we ought to revive that tradition. In this context, many psychologists and psychiatrists are now studying orthodox Jewish child-raising practices because they seem to be so successful. These professionals have concluded that the potent combination of storytelling and highly ritualized celebrations which continue to act out ancient history in contemporary life, work together to provide each new generation with a secure sense of who they are, where they came from, and what is expected of them.

6. *Work hard towards a shared and collaborative ministry structure with all the ways I suggest in my book,* **The Total Parish Manual** *(see bibliography). And then nurture that structure with the means for spiritual development.* Involved parishioners and volunteers are vital, but in light of what we have just read above—and this is crucial—they need formation in order to be effective. This includes spiritual formation, spiritual direction, days of recollection, and so on. This is specially true for full-time laity who work for the church but are not clergy—they were not ordained. These people are not quite laity either because they have a calling and are associated in the eyes of others as being "church people." They need to participate with us in the design of a spirituality that fits a "non-ordained" laity who work for the church. Spiritual direction along with days and evenings of recollection should not only be available but mandatory, built into their yearly schedule.

Be alert to the spiritual needs of your volunteers. There was an article in the April 10th, 1998 issue of the *Wall Street Journal* which noted how highly successful and highly paid executives who have "made it" are finding it empty at the top. As one six-figure broker said, "I thought, 'Here I am, forty-five years old and my life isn't going anyplace. I have a penthouse in Westwood and the right kind of car, and my life is empty.'" So, as the article said, he did something radical: he went back to church. The article goes on: "People in their 40s and 50s are finding themselves at the peak of their careers, wealthy from the stock-market boom—and still feeling there's something missing." So, the man mentioned in the article finally got the nerve to come to the pastor and ask to volunteer and, since he is a top financial whiz, the pastor puts him on the finance committee. Big mistake: what a misreading! The executive does not want to do what he does all day long for a living: he wants God. He wants spirituality, a sense of purpose, of meaning. He's looking for a faith community, greater depth in his life, and God. And what do we offer him? Accounting books.

Spirituality is the groundwork and the basis for faith communities, the glue of the future. Every parish needs spiritual directors available to the people, opportunities for prayer, small faith-sharing groups, Bible study, regularly programmed times of recollection, parish missions, outreach, a rich devotional life, and even an Internet home page before it ever gets to social justice.

And what about the people who have left the church? Most of them are looking for ways to return home. They are looking for a parish with a reputation for hospitality, community, and spirituality, or they are looking for proven reconnecting programs like *Landings* (available from the Paulist fathers; call 1-617-720-5986). Mostly, as all data shows, they are waiting to be asked back.

Recognize the hunger for God in the lives of both parishioners and those who have left the church. And if you don't know what this hunger looks like, read some of the bestselling books on spirituality.

7. *As a practical way of expanding the involvement of all parishioners, practice the "happy endings" format plus personal invitation.* Do not call for volunteers. In other words, cast a wide net. If you place a call for volunteers in the parish bulletin, you can almost predict the names of the people who will step forward, the same old reliable bunch who are always there. And thank God for these people. But the flaw here is that there are other people out there with talent but they will not come forward unless asked. This is where

a personal invitation from the pastor comes in.

To receive a personal letter from the pastor is flattering; even in these days of shared ministry, the mystique of the pastor remains strong. A letter from the pastor infers that he knows me (which is not necessarily true). Further, the recipient of the letter is reluctant to say no to the pastor and, even if that person is not available to volunteer, he or she will at least have to contact the pastor to say so. Finally, a personal invitation reaches out to a wider group and builds community, for at the heart of community is shared experience.

The "happy endings" part means that there should be a time limit placed on office-holding: the presidents of the women's or men's organizations should have a two-year limit; eucharistic ministers and lectors, also two years. (Of course, you can't find volunteer organists all over the place, so the limits there will have to be flexible and reasonable.) These time limits need to be agreed upon up front. By using the "happy endings" method you recycle more people, involve more people, and again, build community. In my previous parish we used this practice with our youth; that is, we invited them to be an usher, a eucharistic minister, or a lector for one month at a particular Mass. By limiting the time involved, the commitment was easy for the teens to handle, and most importantly, it got them involved.

One of the more sensitive issues that comes up frequently in discussions about the church is that there are no younger people taking over the parish ministries. The wonderful people who thirty-five years ago caught the vision of Vatican II, then stepped forward and made the parish and its ministries what they are, are still there. Thirty-five years later the social scene has dramatically changed and the landscape is full of single parents, two-working-parent families, long commutes, work-related travel, the powerful distractions of television and the computer, and other interests and activities. All this leaves people with little time or inclination to get involved in the parish. Yet while this is indeed the reality, we must also admit that there are no mechanisms in place to allow the older people to step down and give others a chance. Indeed, some people don't want to step down. They have invested too much time and energy and sheer devotion to let go. Often, the parish is their life, their social network. They may complain that no one is taking over, but neither do they really want anyone to do so. For the sake of the parish and its people, however, some form of mentoring and outreach must be devised; long-term volunteers and ministers must move on, and new ones encouraged to come in. The "wisdom figures" may stay on as backups, substitutes, teachers, and coworkers, but part of their ministry must be to learn how to recruit, mentor, and replace themselves.

8. *As part of the movement from "in here" to "out there," invite single people to participate in ministry with no strings attached.* There are always single people (like myself) in the parish. Some are well adjusted to social and church life. Others, at times, feel marginal: the never-married, the divorced, the gay or lesbian. Often these people feel cut off from the community, alienated. The wise parish will offer them a public embrace of acceptance by inviting them, through a personal letter, to participate in the liturgy as eucharistic minister, usher, or lector. (Often, a short term commitment—say, three months—is best in these cases.) The symbolism of having people who may be marginalized by their lifestyle or situation standing there openly as a liturgical minister is powerful, compelling, and ultimately moving. The point of this is: what kind of reputation do you want the parish to have? What kind of inclusive community do you want to build? How will you effectively bring the parish to the people?

9. *Foster social justice and outreach but, remember: it must have a spiritual basis.* The parish and its people must indeed

reach out and have a vigorous social agenda, but they must know what they are doing and why. They must return frequently to tap the gospel source of their actions, the inspiration for their commitment, and the motive for their heroism. Otherwise formality and routine will take over and they will wind up as a people "who honor me with their lips but their hearts are far from me."

10. Put the emphasis on events rather than on regular church attendance, especially for youth; this may be more effective in drawing people into the parish. Think of events like the Youth Congress in Denver, work projects away from the parish, fund-raisers for social causes, group neighborhood projects at Christmas, and family Masses that involve both children and parents. Yes, it would be nice if everyone went to church every week (although having Christmas-type participation every weekend might be quite overwhelming!); but the reality is that three-fourths of our Catholics do not attend Mass regularly. Even good Catholics feel no moral compunction about missing Mass now and then. Special events might pave the way for more participation in the parish. Even if not, focusing on special events for all parish constituencies is more in keeping with the rhythms of modern life.

11. Evangelize both the saved—other Catholics—and the unsaved. I refer here to one of the consistent themes in this book: religious illiteracy. It is commonly accepted, as we have seen elsewhere in this book, that Catholics do not know their religion, and they are susceptible to New Age beliefs and fundamentalism for precisely this reason. The church loses one hundred thousand members a day to evangelical Protestantism, largely because Catholics are uninformed about their faith: they can neither explain it nor defend it. On the other hand, the evangelicals are vigorous in their use of propaganda by means of pamphlets, books, radio, and television.

The church must imitate the concentrated, focused, and intense evangelization efforts of the fundamentalists. Catholic parishes should get together to promote Catholic radio talk shows and support the stations that already have them. Another prime spot for evangelization is right between the covers of the phone book. Did you know, for example, that about ninety-five million "hits" per year makes "churches" the thirty-fourth most frequently referenced heading—out of a total of two thousand headings? The yellow pages can be an effective way to get people into church, and a niftily-designed advertisement in the yellow pages would pay off. And don't forget about advertising via local newspapers and supermarkets bulletin boards (but no solicitations, please!).

Speaking of "hits," how about a parish home page on the Internet? Every parish has a whiz kid computer genius who can help to set up a page and solicit services to maintain it. The parish on the Internet, connected by a sophisticated census and chat room, can be powerful in sharing the faith and building community. And as for TV, I have given up in despair and anger at our bishops who have yet to sponsor someone on commercial television. The hunger is there, the audience is there; after all, many Catholics hang onto every word of the Protestant televangelists. While the bishops are looking for the right middle-of-the-road spokesperson, the vacuum of the Catholic presence on television cries to heaven. The title of Marcel Dumestre's book, *A Church At Risk*— at risk from religious illiteracy—is on the mark in defining the problem. As I have said before, we must tap into the places where people are today in order to best reach them.

Concerning the "unsaved," there must be a renewed emphasis on personal visits. This may seem a daunting task, given a dwindling supply of priests and sometimes huge parish rosters. The Protestants and evangelicals use personal visits effectively and with gusto. But most Catholics hate this approach. Like liberal folk, they don't want to "impose" on others: religion is a private thing. Catholics don't want to come on as "holy rollers" or religious fanatics. And, as we have mentioned several times already, they are often not confident that they really know their faith.

Still, good news is good news and to share it is not only a human impulse but the Lord's command as well. There is a middle ground to visitation, a "soft" but effective approach to sharing the faith with people, and this may prove the best way to go for most parishes. Remember, people are hungry for God, and they will gobble up a lot of counterfeit fare if that's all they have available to them. G.K. Chesterton was right: when people cease to believe in something, they do not believe in nothing; they believe in anything.

Somewhere along the line, then, the parish has to create a climate for outreach and evangelization. Laypeople and deacons might work together to develop a program for home visits, with specific time limits laid out for participation (see point 7 above). You may want to refer to resources such as an article by Paulist Father Frank DeSiano in the Spring 1998 issue of *Church* magazine on parish home visitation, which carefully lays out cautions and plans for such a program. Also—and this is important—the parish who is reaching out to people wisely seeds the various neighborhoods and housing developments with formation people and/or trained leaders. These people provide ongoing services for faith development, such as Bible study or faith-sharing groups, as well as keep an eye on the needs of people and report on these needs to the parish staff.

12. *Offer people a deeper and more personal way to become members of the parish by developing a better joining process.* Most people join a parish in this way: someone drops into the office, asks the secretary for a form, fills it out, makes sure the kids get into CCD, and then drives off into the sunset. The problems with this method are many. First, no one

except the secretary has met the new people. They leave no trace of themselves except for a brief record on a large index card. Second, the pastor doesn't know who they are, nor have they met him. Third, what do they know about the parish, its philosophy, its spirituality, its expectations? Probably nothing. Finally, they have had no exposure to what is available—and asked of them—in terms of commitment and service in the parish.

In my previous parish, we developed a very satisfying way for new people to come into the parish. When they approach the already-overworked secretary, they are simply given a little pamphlet whose cover page reads:

> Seeking Partnership with St. Mary's Parish: You have requested membership in St. Mary's Parish. We are pleased to consider you and delighted that you asked. Please read the enclosed information and, after you do so, call our welcoming chairpersons and they will start you on your way.
>
> —The St. Mary's Parish Council

First, notice the change of language; from "joining" (like joining the Kiwanis) to "seeking partnership" and "faith community." That puts potential parishioners on the alert. They then read that joining is not automatic, but under "consideration"; this is a real eye-opener for most people. Inside the little pamphlet readers find out that the joining process consists of three sessions with various parish members.

Session one is called "Crossing the Jordan," a reference to ancient Israel where those seeking conversion to the Hebrew faith had to undergo an exodus experience. Since the Jewish converts had not been present when the Israelites had passed over the waters of the Jordan into the Promised Land, they had to do this symbolically by reentering Israel's history through its founding Scriptures. Likewise, prospective parishioners who have not experienced the founding event of St. Mary's Parish enter into our story through an explanation of both the history of our beginnings and the philosophy that has defined us as a parish of shared, collaborative ministry. Thus, this first session is dedicated to the story of how we came to be, who we are, and what drives us as a parish.

Session two is titled "Ministries." St. Mary's Parish tries to meet many needs, and so has many ministries. Along with this, there is a certain spirit at St. Mary's, a way we feel about God and each other, a way we celebrate, worship, and support one another. The second section covers the functioning of the various parish ministries, as well as the spirit and celebrations of our faith community. The third and final session is on spirituality.

When someone has completed all three sessions, a covenant is signed between the new parishioner and the parish community. On this covenant is a place for the person to make a commitment to some service to the community, as well as a place where a family photograph can be glued. (We also make copies of this photograph for the church bulletin board and the parish bulletin, asking the rest of the parish to welcome the newcomers when they see them.) Although laypeople from the parish run each of the sessions, the pastor is present at all of them. This way everyone gets to know and recognize one another. As a final step in the joining process, once a year we gather all who have joined the parish in the past year for a family party and reinforcement of their covenant.

I am sure you will agree that all of this is not simply signing up to join a parish: this is a process of entrance into a community. For some this process may sound like one more burden on the people, one more rule. But surely part of reclaiming some sort of Catholic identity involves making demands. The gospels are replete with the theme of discipleship, and discipleship makes demands of Christians. Demands are an accepted part of modern secular life. Obstetricians require their patients to go to a six-week Lamaze class. The Boy Scouts demand that certain tasks be fulfilled to obtain a merit badge. If a child wants to play sports they—and their parents—must come to meetings and practices and commit to lots of afternoons and weekends of blood, sweat, and tears. The road to Carnegie Hall is long and arduous (practice, practice, practice!). By nature, most people are willing to pay a price for what they want: what comes too easily is not valued. You take a year off after you graduate college to teach in the inner city school where the recruiter told you it was dangerous and three teachers lost their lives in the past five years. The parish sponsors trips to Appalachia or supports the Jesuit Volunteer Program because affluent middle-class Christians need to experience the Christ who is "out there." People want a challenge, they really do. Why are we afraid to give it?

Ironically, the many Catholics who join fundamentalist groups, the very ones who moaned if the homily was too long and the Mass exceeded forty minutes, are the ones who now spend four hours at Wednesday night Bible study, tithe, adopt a strict moral code, and hit the streets to evangelize. The criticism of demands, of course, usually concerns the manner of presentation. If you give a dictatorial fiat from above—this is it, or else!—people will be turned off. On the other hand, if the demands are part of the policy of a reflective community that feeds the need for commitment and the desperate hunger for God, then people will be eager to comply. The truth is, the people who participate in the process of joining St. Mary's have been quite delighted with the experience. For many, it is the first time they have a chance to listen to what "parish" means, to find out what a faith community might look like. It is a chance to ask questions, as well as meet other parishioners and the pastor.

13. *Pay attention to the men.* Many have spoken of the feminization of the church, where women now predominate in the structure as well as in the spirit. Their presence is felt as teachers, DREs, pastoral associates, eucharistic ministers, lectors, chancellors, tribunal judges, and the like. Coupled with our capitalistic system which removes many males from the scene by keeping them at work for long hours, along with widespread divorce and high mobility, there is indeed a gap for male participation in the church. The men need a forum. Remember, the founder of the Promise Keepers is a former Catholic. I have found that an early morning time—6:30 AM, perhaps, before the workday begins—can be a good time for men to gather for Mass, shared prayer (using one of the hours in the Divine Office, for example), or Bible study.

14. *Customize the liturgy to fit the needs of the parish, at least occasionally.* This could mean offering a short Mass for the hurried, a Mass of medium length for the interested, and for the thoughtful, a long, well-prepared, celebratory liturgy with dialogue and powerful music. After all, how many opportunities are there for people to process the homily, much less to respond or challenge—with coffee and cake afterwards, of course. These folk will be the searchers, the seekers after spirituality, the returnees, the salt.

15. *Somehow, we have to fill the desperate need to coherently reinterpret the faith for a people for whom the church has lost all credibility.* This credibility has been lost not only in the church's political and social stances, but in its very beliefs. This gets a little rarefied, but, as an expression of the problem, attend to the words of Catholic historian Eamon Duffy:

> At the beginning of this century it is not too much to claim that the greatest intellectual challenge facing the Christian church was precisely the burden of history. The emergence of scientific history had disenchanted the past, and had

posed with an immediacy never before known, a series of questions which highlighted the apparent gulf between faith and fact. As source criticism, textual criticism, historical criticism turned the microscope and the dissecting knife on the texts of sacred Scripture, the gospels seemed to dwindle from timeless utterances of the Holy Spirit to the laborious works of name- less editors, aimed very specifically at first-cen- tury audiences in Antioch, Rome, or the Hellenic Jewish diaspora.

And with the relativising of the gospels came the reduction to human proportions of their central figure. At the very moment when histor- ical criticism began that great if reluctant redis- covery of the Jewishness of Jesus, which is our century's most remarkable contribution to the doctrine of Christ, the very presuppositions of that doctrine came to seem less credible. How could a wandering first-century apocalyptic prophet from one of the least savoury outposts of the Roman world be taken seriously as the eternal Word of God? Was not the whole fabric of Nicene Christianity, its imaginings of the tri- une life of God projected into the obscure and sordid history of first-century Palestine, a fanta- sy, the hopeless Hellenizing of an utterly differ- ent Jewish original? The search for the historical Jesus seemed to call into question the whole weight and direction of subsequent Christian history (*The Tablet,* July 4, 1998).

Educated Catholics must deal with this "apparent gulf between fact and faith." It does no good to take the stance of some who are fearful of the domino effect: for example, if they acknowledge the fact that Jesus really didn't say some of the words put into his mouth, then what else of the gospels was made up? Even more, could someone have made up the whole Jesus story? So, these fearful people conclude that you must read Scripture literally and accept the infancy narratives as objectively true or the whole fabric falls apart. There are some who say that St. Paul (and even perhaps Jesus himself) was decidedly wrong about the end of the world coming in his lifetime or soon thereafter; this leads to the question, what else was Paul wrong about? If the New Testament—significantly, all but one of its twenty-seven books was written outside Palestine, the land of Jesus—is the interpretative product of the early church and not the recordings of eyewitnesses, how reliable is it? Questions such as these force the issue of how we can intelligently and coherently reinterpret our timeless faith with the findings of modern science. How do we forge a catechesis that respects modern science and at the same time embraces a tradition?

Of course, none of this challenge is made easier by the polarization that exists between conservative and liberal Catholics, and the lack of any common ground between them. The trouble is that each side wants its own extremes taught as absolute, unchanging doctrine. The conservatives want to uphold the pope's right to appoint bishops. The liberals want democratic elections. But as we saw back in chapter seven, the pope's privilege of episcopal appointments is a novelty; historically, the people presented the candidates for bishop. Surely there is room for a middle ground of popularly chosen episcopal candidates for Rome to approve and appoint. The conservatives want an "all-or-nothing" profession of faith as the criterion of a good Catholic, while the liberals are dubbed "cafeteria" Catholics. The middle ground here acknowledges the traditional, time-honored hierarchy of truths: not all teachings have equal value or equal demands on assent. The conservatives want a no-questions-asked, full obedience to strict, top-down hierarchical directives from the magisterium. The liberals want everything discussed and challenged. The middle ground is to admit the existence of authoritarianism as well as of doctrinal anarchy. Clearly, dealing with the polarization of the church is a twenty-first century challenge to the intellect, good will, and, most of all, the imagination of all Catholics.

16. *The parish must forthrightly change its vision of itself as a successful enterprise.* Because we live in a capitalistic culture, the language of corporate goals and practices has crept into our mission as a church. Being well-organized and seeing itself as part of a larger institution are important to the parish, but not primary. That the pastor be a good administrator and clerical CEO is important to the parish, but not primary. What is most important to the parish, or should be, is the spiritual life of its parishioners. The parish, simply put, must teach people how to pray, how to read the mystics, how to read the Bible, and how to meditate. It should provide opportunities for spiritual direction, and offer retreats both at the parish and elsewhere. It should be ecumenical in its approach. Of utmost importance is training people in the regular practice of the spiritual exercises. The parish as "place" has to give way to the parish as "seeking"; good works, a strong community, and social justice will flow from that perspective. I don't know how they train seminarians these days, but it seems to me that training in spiritual guidance should be rigorous because that is what the parish of the future needs most.

Spirituality and Tradition

When you add up the sixteen suggestions mentioned in this chapter, they all come down to this: spirituality within the framework of communal belief. Yet spirituality itself is not enough. If it is to transcend personal experience, it needs the context of a community; it needs to be part of a shared story. Therefore, spirituality needs the church as much as the church needs it. This connection is important because the tendency to fall under the spell of a charismatic leader is strong and separatism is always a temptation. We need the strong formation of many small groups of counterculture disciples united through the bishops to the core tradition.

And indeed we must first look into our own tradition before we converse with others. At the same time, we must be open to other traditions for the simple fact is that religion is now a pluralistic enterprise. So we must be open to the wisdom and the experiences and the stories of others, but we must do so from our own base. Pluralism does not mean being open to all traditions except your own. As Andrew Greeley puts it, "One who does not know where one stands, stands nowhere." He continues:

> There can be no objection to those who are interested in Asian mysticism if first they have explored the mysticism of their own heritage. Explore all you want in Indian mysticism, so long as in your search you don't forget about the Anglo-Saxon mystics—Rolle, Hilton (that is not a hotel), Julianna, and the author of the *Cloud of Unknowing*, to say nothing of Piers Plowman. Be you Catholic and you plumb Buddhist mystics without first paying some attention to Juan DeLa Cruz, you have alienated yourself from your own roots. You can't learn from others unless you learn first from who and what you are. Only teenagers, and shallow ones at that, may be excused for turning against all that shaped them. (from a paper given at a conference at the University of California at Santa Barbara)

The mention of bishops brings me to a final comment. I don't know how much control we have here, but I suggest we need a new breed of leaders, a new breed of bishops. We surely need those who defend orthodoxy and fundamental institutional concerns. But such things should be important, not primary. We need people who will lead not from the top but from the trenches, especially those gifted ones all over this country (and there are many of them, usually unsung outside their communities, often unaffirmed by their bishops), who are doing extraordinary things and building vibrant faith communities. Leaders should come from those who admire and promote the Vatican II parishes being formed throughout the country, even if they can't emulate this themselves.

What's needed is really a different mindset, a biblical sense of community and justice, a Christlike empathy for the marginal and downtrodden, a feel for the people. We need leaders who are willing to take chances; whose pastoral concerns and decisions dominate the marketplace; who know we are in a different time and a different place and a different century; who know that the gospel has to be recreated all over again, just as it has always been throughout history. These leaders must grasp the reality that since the 1990s, there are more laypeople (most of them women) in graduate theology and ministry programs than young men studying for the priesthood, and that because they will increasingly be working side by side to reshape the clerical culture they must be introduced to each other early on in their formal training.

I could go from coast to coast citing examples of servant leaders who are doing extraordinary things, but most of you will not have heard of these people. Instead let me return to a high profile person, one even mentioned as being the next pope. Let me return to Cardinal Martini of Milan, whose words ended our chapter on Apocalyptic times. He is a shining example of a bishop for the next millennium. For example, he regularly invites people belonging to every religion, or even no religion at all, to gather at the cathedral in his diocese to share why they believe as they do (or why they do not believe at all). His reasoning is this: why not give an open voice to this inner struggle by listening to all people who are in search of meaning? He has invited Marxist philosophers, psychiatrists, artists, and poets to speak about the search for a meaning to life. Normally, between one and two thousand people participate. Cardinal Martini has no hidden agenda. He simply wants to offer people a chance to think and reflect on what life means. He goes on to say:

> One time, a group of young people asked me to explain to them how to pray with the Bible, which I did. Approximately two hundred of us stayed up the better part of one evening—I remember we were outdoors on a delightful May night sitting on the grass. I explained something about prayer in the Bible. Some of them asked me to give an example of practical biblical prayer. I did so. As we continued our sessions, we moved into the cathedral since our number had grown to more than five hundred, a thousand, two, three, four thousand, until each month the cathedral was full. (*America*, May 2, 1998)

Again, we see that persistent hunger for God. Remember Damien Thompson's words: "The populations of North America and Europe are torn between a new materialism and an intense yearning for the sacred." We need leaders who are not only sensitive to that hunger but will feed it, leaders who know how to respond to the yearning. Bureaucrats and power people need not apply.

Closing Perspectives

We have examined the New Age, fundamentalism, and millennium intricacies. We have looked at the decline of the Total Church and have made some suggestions on shaping a new Catholic identity. We have noted the measurable falling-off of church attendance, the prevalence of the secular mentality, and, for Catholics, sharp disagreement in the areas of sex and authority. These last two areas are intertwined because, in spite of high expectations and indications otherwise, the birth control encyclical entered every Catholic bedroom in America and was largely rejected, along with the authority that issued the ban to begin with. Today, the fallout from this disagreement is seen among young Catholics, only a quarter of whom, according to Andrew Greeley, have any confidence in the church, and only seven percent of whom believe that premarital sex is wrong.

Still, there is good news. The proportion of Catholics in the overall population remains pretty much the same as it was at the beginning of this century; belief in an afterlife has increased since that time; and there has been no massive apostasy from the church's doctrine. Religion, in fact, remains an important aspect of people's lives, and in spite of global attempts at secularization, the interest in spirituality is at an all-time high. Those culture wars we spoke of in chapter seven are really more skirmishes among the intellectual elite and are of little concern to the general population. Think of the massive failure of the liberal group Call to Action, who sought one million signatures on a petition for reform but only got thirty-seven thousand: the average Catholic's interest lies elsewhere.

The religious impulse has motivated large moral movements for better or worse: think of abolition, prohibition, and the civil rights movement. Further, think of the new sensitivity to ecology, feminism, and the spiritual life. In spite of seemingly high rates of divorce, most people want to be married. Fidelity is not obsolete, and people are not as selfish as they are sometimes portrayed. Americans give a higher proportion of their income to charity and are more likely to volunteer than any other people in the world; in fact, volunteering has increased in the eighties and nineties. New Age, fundamentalism, and endtime scripts are all covert signs of this basic goodness and cryptic yearning for the divine, the numinous. We've been there. We are there. We have much to offer.

Let's come back, then, to what I said at the beginning: the image of the modern parish is no longer the church in the middle of the rural village, and the lives of the parishioners no longer conform to the rhythms of the seasons. No, the parish is, realistically, *one of many* claims on people's lives; for many, it holds the least claim. Its role, therefore, is much more humble: to be a center of formation, hospitality, healing, and worship, in service to people whose lives are global, fast-paced, and secularized, who live in the world and must find salvation there, and who for all their activity and stimulation, for all their affluence and endless choices, feel a deep hunger and a profound sense that all is not well. We need to restore our confidence in the fact that, after all, we have a two-thousand year heritage. We have the Spirit of Jesus. We have tradition and history. We have the Good News. Remember, there are still some thirty million Catholics who attend Mass regularly and therefore still constitute the single largest denomination in the United States.

Let me close appropriately, then, by once more quoting author Charles Morris, who in his odyssey across the country observed:

> At the grassroots I was very pleasantly surprised. There are clearly some things one would worry about but there's not much of a crisis. Granted I was looking mostly at the good parishes but I also visited "bad" parishes. I mean

that I asked people who had "parish shopped" where they had come from, then I visited those parishes. I went to five Masses a weekend for a while...I would time travel back in my head to what parishes had been like in the fifties. While everyone today talks about what bad preachers priests are, I remember when I was younger that priests didn't even try to preach.

Most of the priests I saw on my visits were trying. They had thought about their homilies and the Masses were participatory. Even the poorly-rated parishes weren't so bad. And the good parishes seemed to be running along the way the Vatican II people hoped they might, with a lot of energy and participation. I sat in on a number of parish council meetings and was impressed by how smart the lay people were and how much they knew about the church.

New Age, fundamentalism, apocalypticism, collapse of the total parish—they and other factors have brought us low and made us small. But take notice: low as a foot-washer and small as a mustard seed.

Select Bibliography

Bausch, William J. *The Total Parish Manual* (Twenty-Third Publications, 1995).

Carpenter, Joel. *Revive Us Again: The Reawakening of American Fundamentalism* (Oxford University Press).

Boyer, Paul. *When Time Shall Be No More* (Belknap, Harvard, 1992).

Cahill, Thomas. *How the Irish Saved Civilization* (Doubleday, 1995).

Cuneo, Michael W. *The Smoke of Satan* (Oxford University Press, 1997).

Epperly, Bruce. *Crystal and Cross* (Twenty-Third Publications, 1996).

Dumestre, Marcel J. *A Church at Risk* (Crossroad, 1997).

Ellis, Richard. *Imagining Atlantis* (Alfred A. Knopf, 1998).

Fergenson, Duncan, ed. *New Age Spirituality: An Assessment* (WJKP, 1993).

Fletcher, Richard. *The Barbarian Conversion* (Henry Holt, 1988).

Gallagher, Michael Paul, S.J. *Clashing Symbols* (Paulist Press, 1998).

Grootius, Douglas. *Confronting the New Age: How to Resist a Growing Religious Movement* (IVP, 1988).

Hahn, Scott and Kimberly. *Rome Sweet Rome* (Ignatius Press, 1993).

Kingwell, Mark. *Dreams of Millennium: Report from a Culture on the Brink* (Faber and Faber).

LeBar, James. *Cults, Sects and the New Age* (Our Sunday Visitor, 1989).

Marty and Appleby. *The Glory and the Power* (Beacon Press, 1992).

Melton, James and Louis. *Perspectives on the New Age* (SUNY Press, 1992).

Morris, Charles R. *American Catholic* (Times Books, Random House,1997).

Pable, Martin. *Catholics and Fundamentalists* (ACTA Publications, 1991).

Paqua, Mitch, S.J. *Catholics and the New Age* (Servant, 1992).

Peter, Ted. *The Cosmic Self: A Penetrating Look at Today's New Age Movements* (Harper 1991).

Saliba, John. *Understanding the New Religious Movements,* (Eerdmans, 1996).

Stackhouse, Reginald. *The End of the World? A New Look at an Old Belief* (Paulist, 1997).

Stark, Rodney. *The Rise of Christianity* (Harper, 1997).

Thompson, Damien. *The   of Time* (University of New England, 1996).